Above: The emblem of the London, Midland & Scottish Railway.
Crown Copyright, National Railway Museum, York

Below: A cameo from a Midland Railway press advertisement
of 1922. *BR*

policy of the new LMS were to be seen at the British
Empire Exhibitions of 1924 and 1925 at Wembley.
Thus the largest railway group exhibiting had to be
content with an inside-cylindered Bowen-Cooke 4-6-0
No 5845 with outside valve gear, the only member of
its class built by the LMS and temporarily named
Prince of Wales, and a Hughes 4-6-4T No 11114 in
crimson lake livery. Neither was exactly representative
of a railway with over 10,000 locomotives, and I must
admit it puzzled me at the time.

However it must have been symptomatic of what
was going on behind the scenes, for George Hughes
the first Chief Mechanical Engineer of the LMS retired
in 1925. A Lancashire & Yorkshire man, he was
succeeded by Sir Henry Fowler of the Midland.
However one major legacy of the Horwich regime was
to appear, the excellent 2-6-0 'Crabs', some of whose
virtues were to be incorporated in the equally successful 2-6-4Ts. However Fowler found himself faced with
the same difficulties that Hughes had encountered, an
over powerful motive power department under a
former Midland man, James Anderson. The philos-

7

Above: A cameo from a LMS press advertisement of 1925. *BR*

ophy of the small engine policy which had generally worked so well on the MR, was to cause considerable difficulty when applied in the wider context of the LMS. For all that, the standardisation and economy of the existing Derby designs gave good service for a time, and particularly the Compounds or 'crimson ramblers' as they came to be known.

By the late 1920s heavy loadings, particularly on the West Coast route brought matters to a head, and with the aid of the North British Locomotive Co, the powerful 3-cylinder 4-6-0 'Royal Scots' appeared in 1927 in a hurry which later produced teething problems. However they were an immediate success, and again using three cylinders Fowler set about rebuilding the LNW 'Claughtons' into a completely new class of engines, which became known as 'Baby Scots', but were officially called 'Patriots'. The first two prototypes appeared from Derby in 1930 and heralded the beginnings of another successful class.

When Sir Henry Fowler left in 1931, he was followed for a short time by E. H. J. Lemon, the Carriage & Wagon Superintendent. In 1932, William Stanier from Swindon was appointed to be the new Chief Mechanical Engineer, and it was he who was able to weld together the individual loyalties of Derby, Crewe and Horwich.

Therefore the 1930s became the 'bright morning' of Stanier's locomotives, many of which, apart from his Pacifics, were based on Fowler engines, but used Swindon ideas. Not all of the latter were applicable as he discovered in the case of the early 3-cylinder 'Jubilee' 4-6-0s, which at first were not as good steamers as their 'Patriot' predecessors. However his

2-cylinder 4-6-0s introduced at the same time, the famous 'Black Fives', proved to be one of the most popular and useful types of locomotive ever to run in Britain. All three classes became mainstays of the Midland Division, together with the 4-4-0 Compounds.

Only occasionally in the early days after the amalgamation was the Midland image at St Pancras disturbed by the visit of a North Western 'Prince' or 'Claughton'. A North Staffordshire 0-6-2T is reputed to have worked there, and there are unconfirmed reports of Hughes 4-6-4Ts. A variation in Midland type locomotives was provided by some Deeley 0-6-4Ts, more at home in the Midlands, and 'Tilbury' 4-6-4Ts and 4-4-2Ts. The new Fowler engines continued the Derby tradition. It was still basically a Midland scene.

In 1934, just as Stanier's new locomotives were coming into service, I became a season ticket holder on the Midland main line, travelling daily between Radlett, a village just below St Albans, and St Pancras. Some of the personal memories and photographs in this book are centred around that end of the line, others go north to Derby, north-west to Belfast, and into the eastern counties. I found the 1930s of great interest, I hope you will too.

Acknowledgements
I would like to express my gratitude to Mr H. C. Casserley, Mr C. R. L. Coles, Mr T. J. Edgington Technical Information Officer National Railway Museum, Mr S. G. Morrison Librarian Institution of Mechanical Engineers, Mr B. Stephenson and others who have helped in the preparation of this book.

Alan Whitehead MSIAD

BRISTOL — BATH

Burnham on Sea
Highbridge
Radstock
Wells
EVERCREECH JN
Bridgewater Glastonbury
Wincanton
Templecombe
Blandford
Wimborne
BROADSTONE JN.

HUMBER

S & D J R (MID-LSWR)

BOURNEMOUTH

ington
PTON
Ilkley
MID-NE Otley
Yeadon
LEEDS

Dewsbury
Normanton
Knottingley
SFIELD
BARNSLEY
MID-NE
Swinton
SHEFFIELD ROTHERHAM
Hope
Worksop Retford
NLEY
S Dore
Chester
-field
LINCOLN
ll Mansfield
Matlock
sworth Newark
Ilkeston
DERBY NOTTINGHAM
Trent Melton Mowbray
Trent
Lough-
borough Bourne
Ashby
de-la-Zouch Coalville Stamford
Spalding
Tamworth Oakham Wisbech
LEICESTER
MID-WNT Wigston PETERBOROUGH
NUNEATON
Market
Harborough
Hampton Loddington KETTERING Thrapston
Green RUGBY
Wellingborough GE
Higham Huntingdon
NORTHAMPTON Ferrers
CAMBRIDGE
BEDFORD

Hitchin

Luton
Harpenden
St Albans
Hemel Hempstead Radlett
Romford
Cricklewood Upminster Pitsea
BRENT JN LTSR(MR) SOUTHEND
ST PANCRAS Grays Shoeburyness
FFNCHURCH ST Tilbury

Melton
Constable Cromer
Fakenham
North
Walsham
M&GN
KINGS LYNN
(South Lynn) GREAT
YARMOUTH
NORWICH
GE M&GN
Lowestoft

MIDLAND RAILWAY
PRE LMSR

89

11 NOV 1989

PTW

THE MIDLAND IN THE 1930s

Please renew/return this item by the last date shown.

So that your telephone call is charged at local rate, please call the numbers as set out below:

	From Area codes 01923 or 020:	From the rest of Herts:
Renewals:	01923 471373	01438 737373
Enquiries:	01923 471333	01438 737333
Textphone:	01923 471599	01438 737599

L32   www.hertsdirect.org/librarycatalogue

THE MIDLAND IN THE 1930s

ALAN WHITEHEAD

IAN ALLAN LTD
LONDON

For
Victor F. Whitehead

First published 1982

ISBN 0 7110 1202 4

Published by Ian Allan Ltd, Shepperton, Surrey;
and printed by Ian Allan Printing Ltd at their works
at Coombelands in Runnymede, England

Contents

Introduction   6
The St Pancras Line   9
Sheds Along the Line   51
Iron Horses at Derby   75
Down the Thames Estuary   91
Into East Anglia   105
Northern Ireland   109

*It has been a conscious decision to include in this volume
photographs of historic interest which might, in other conditions,
have been excluded on grounds of quality. It is hoped that the reader
will accept the consequent reduction in the production standards of
some plates.*

Bibliography
Reference has been made to the following in the
compilation of this volume.
Casserley, H. & Dorman C.; *Midland Album*;
Ian Allan Ltd.

Casserley, H. & Johnston S.; *Locomotives at the
Grouping 3*; Ian Allan Ltd.

Cox E.; *Locomotive Panorama Vol 1*; Ian Allan Ltd.

Dow G. & Lacy R.; *Midland Style*;
Historical Model Railway Society.

Leech K.; *Tilbury Tanks Loco Profile 27*;
Profile Publications Ltd.

Hamilton Ellis C.; *The Midland Railway*;
Ian Allan Ltd.

Haresnape B.; *Fowler Locomotives*; Ian Allan Ltd.

Haresnape B.; *Stanier Locomotives*; Ian Allan Ltd.

Jenkinson D.; *An Illustrated History of LNW
Coaches*; Oxford Publishing Co.

Lake G.; *The Railways of Tottenham*;
Greenlake Publications Ltd.

Radford J.; *Derby Works and Midland Locos*;
Ian Allan Ltd.

Stephenson B.; *LMS Album 2 and 3*; Ian Allan Ltd.

Atkins C.; *'Fury* on Trial'; *Railway Magazine*
December 1978.

Weatherburn R.; 'Leaves from the Log of a
Locomotive Engineer'; *Railway Magazine*
December 1912

Introduction

As I was born just before World War 1, I was able as a boy to see something of the old companies before they were swallowed up into four large groups in 1923. The transition to the London, Midland & Scottish Railway seemed to have little effect on the Midland — the livery remained and most new locomotives continued Derby practice, just as carriage design apart from sleeping cars was in the Midland tradition. For other constituents of the group it was not so easy, the powerful North Western in particular found the change traumatic. This I can understand, even now in my memories of youth I can recall a black 4-6-0 'Prince' at Euston, backing on to a train of coaches resplendent in that famous colour scheme of spilt milk and purple brown. Such glory was to pass.

Although one is inclined to think of the Railways Act of 1921, which resulted in the 1923 amalgamation as something imposed by Government, the actual form the grouping took stemmed from a paper produced by the Railway Companies' Association, with the North Eastern a notable dissentient. The RCA document envisaged four main groups (plus provision for London), whose composition virtually coincided with what finally took place. The Government White Paper of 1920, had proposed smaller groupings: Southern, Western, North Western, Eastern, North Eastern, Scottish and one for London. The North Western combination would have been the LNW, Midland, Lancashire & Yorkshire, North Staffordshire and Furness. In restrospect, the Government scheme with its smaller groupings might have led to an easier birth, especially in the locomotive and carriage departments of the railways concerned.

The uncertainties surrounding the future locomotive

Left: The wyvern, emblem of the Midland Railway and displayed throughout the system.
Crown Copyright, National Railway Museum, York

The St Pancras Line

Although the Midland became a major railway in the 1840s, as far as London was concerned it was still a provincial system with Derby as its centre. In one sense this always remained true, for although it became one of the largest railways in the United Kingdom, and its eventual impact on the capital was memorable, London never appeared on its coat-of-arms alongside the cities of Birmingham, Derby, Bristol, Leicester, Lincoln and Leeds. Although the railway became a national institution, Derby remained the seat of power for administration, operation and motive power and the principal officers were located there.

The Midland's earliest contact with the metropolis was via the London & North Western at Rugby, whilst its link at Normanton with the York & North Midland and thence the York, Newcastle & Berwick and North British Railways made it part of an early East Coast route to Scotland. This was some two years before the Great Northern opened up its line from the south which led to the eventual East Coast association.

However the appearance of the Great Northern provided a possible alternative to Euston as an outlet to the capital. In 1857 a line, laid with double-headed 80lb rails and inside-keyed, was built by the Midland from Leicester, through Bedford to join the Great Northern at Hitchin. The desired access to Kings Cross did not come easily however, as an existing agreement with the LNW had first to be declared invalid in the law courts, strongly contested needless to say by the powers at Euston.

For a time the Midland was linked with both Euston and Kings Cross, in fact the former station still had the best trains including the night mail, but they were worked with LNW engines and guards as far as Rugby. However with Kings Cross the Midland had running powers for both goods and passenger trains, its own rented round house — known as the Derby shed — for its engines at the terminus, and a special booking office for its passengers.

However it was human nature for the Great Northern to look after its own traffic first and the resulting delays to Midland trains from the congestion that gradually built up proved so unsatisfactory that in a little over 10 years Derby had opened its own line from Bedford to the south. This time heavier 83lb double-headed rails were laid, but still with inside-

Left: An engraved view of St Pancras station exterior from Ward Lock's guide to London of 1880.
Ward Lock & Co Ltd

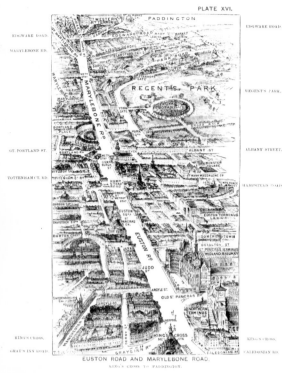

PLATE XVI.

EUSTON ROAD AND MARYLEBONE ROAD.
KING'S CROSS TO PADDINGTON.

Derby's contribution to the London scene had an impact which can be seen in the Victorian painting in the Museum of London by J. O'Connor entitled *Horse trams on Pentonville Hill*. In spite of the title it is the spires and roof of the station that caught the artist's imagination. Within this vast railway 'cathedral' (there is a story that an American worshipper went there instead of to St Pancras Church), the ethos of the steam railway could be fully sensed. Smoke and steam ascending to a sky which was the roof, the whistles and rhythmic exhausts of departing trains, the insistent clang of a bell as a number slid into the face of the great clock, giving the platform of the next arrival — all these form impressions that are not easily forgotten.

The London Extension, as it was called, passed through pleasant countryside up to Cricklewood, then called Childs Hill. A pattern of local train services evolved from the rural into a timetable that met the needs of the growth in population between Bedford and London. As the number of passengers and season ticket holders increased, so outer suburban trains tended to terminate farther down the line. After Hendon came Radlett, then St Albans, next Harpenden and Luton. In the up direction in addition to St Pancras, at Kentish Town trains could descend to the Metropolitan widened lines to terminate at Moorgate, or connections could be made with the services to South Tottenham, East Ham and Barking, linking up there with the Tilbury and Southend line.

Motive power for the local services in the earlier days was provided by Kirtley well-tank and Johnson 0-4-4Ts hauling sets of four-wheelers, six-wheelers and by 1911 close coupled formations of bogie stock. Kirtley and Johnson 2-4-0s appeared both on these, and the express services where they were joined by the Johnson 4-4-0s and the 'singles'. Until about 1900 there were six Beyer Peacock Metropolitan type condensing 4-4-0T engines on local services which the Midland had acquired for the Moorgate lines, receiving as the years went by, Derby boilers and other features.

I was a week-end visitor to St Pancras in the 1920s, but by the 1930s when the Midland had been a part of the London, Midland & Scottish Railway for some 10 years, I started to travel into and out of St Pancras daily. Radlett was $15\frac{1}{4}$ miles down the main line from the terminus, and its church had the distinction of having been built with the aid of funds collected for the spiritual welfare of the railway navvies engaged in the construction of the London Extension. Radlett's station served a growing village, sported displays of flowers on the platforms, and had just become the scene of an LMS experiment in brighter decor. This consisted of emerald green, orange and other colours, and a new design of name-board. In the sidings parallel with the

keyed track. The new line passed through the straw hat manufacturing town of Luton, the city of St Albans with its great Norman cathedral, the villages of Radlett, Hendon and Childs Hill to its own terminus at St Pancras, above and beside the station of its former GN partner.

The capital was now connected directly with the heart of the Midland system at Derby and all the ramifications of this large and important railway. A worthy triumphal arch was provided. It is said that barrels of Burton beer gave the basic measure for the terminus! Be that as it may, the resulting train shed was a magnificent expression of Victorian engineering. William Barlow's masterpiece was followed later by a soaring Gothic style hotel, whose architect Sir Gilbert Scott described as 'possibly too good for its purpose'. Scott had no reason to regret his design for with his Midland Grand Hotel, he had provided London with one of its finest buildings in Victorian Gothic.

The theme had already been anticipated by the Midland consulting engineer William Barlow in the slightly pointed arch formed by the great cast-iron roof of his train shed, soaring itself 100ft above the rails, with a clear span of 240ft. At the time it was the widest cast-iron span that had been built anywhere in the world. On 1 October 1868 trains ran into the still unfinished terminus for the first time.

10

up slow platform were still some interesting remnants of the old Midland inside-keyed track.

My up trains in the morning were the 7.53 non-stop, the 8.1 stopping or the 8.18 semi-fast. The 'St Pancras only' and the semi-fast were hauled by the Fowler 2-6-4Ts or the Stanier 3-cylinder taper boiler version introduced in 1934 and eventually destined for the Southend line. My up stopping trains were usually worked by the Fowler condensing 2-6-2Ts.

Having departed eight minutes earlier from St Albans, the 7.53am picked up only at Radlett and with tare loads ranging between 89 and 90 tons, plus passengers, depending on the three or four-coach set used, this well patronised train was a real flyer. With a schedule of 18 minutes for the 15¼ miles to St Pancras, including a climb of 1 in 200 up to Elstree, there was

no time for loitering especially when the occasional check could be anticipated outside the terminus. One of the best runs I had with this train was with Fowler 2-6-4T No 2327 with a load of 89 tons tare, which in spite of two checks did the journey to St Pancras in 17min 4sec.

In the evenings down to Radlett my journeys centred on the 6.47pm train, stopping only at Mill Hill and Elstree. With a steady climb most of the way to Cricklewood and then between Hendon and Elstree, ranging between 1 in 168 and 176, with loads of seven to eight carriages giving a total of 170 to 186 tons tare, the 2-6-4Ts gave a good account of themselves. It was a favourite roster for No 2300, the first of the class built at Derby in 1927, the 31-minute schedule often being cut to 29 or 30 minutes. My other trains were the 7.53pm, stopping at the same stations, but with a timing of 33 minutes, usually a Johnson 0-4-4T or Fowler 2-6-2T turn; the 8.45pm, stopping additionally at Cricklewood, normally a 2-6-2T roster; and the 9.20pm all stations, which usually had a 2-6-4T. On Saturdays the 1.25pm to Bedford with a timing of 30 minutes to Radlett, stopping at Mill Hill and Elstree on the way, was usually a 4-4-0 Compound turn worked by one of Nos 1003/35/40-3/91/9. Occasionally a Stanier 'Jubilee' 4-6-0 would take over, such as No 5663 *Jervis* or No 5664 *Nelson*.

In the 1920s and early 1930s at St Pancras

C. 35

CHEAP TICKETS
DAILY
TO AND FROM
ALL STATIONS
BETWEEN

MOORGATE

| ST. PANCRAS | BARKING |
| EAST HAM | ST. ALBANS |

HEMEL HEMPSTED

| LUTON | BEDFORD |

AND INTERMEDIATE STATIONS

AVAILABILITY OF TICKETS.

OUTWARD.—Week-days.—By any train except the following:—
    7.25 a.m., Bedford to St. Pancras.
    7.57 a.m., Luton to St. Pancras.
    8.10 a.m., Harpenden to St. Pancras.

RETURN.—By any train on day of issue of ticket.

FIRST CLASS CHEAP TICKETS ARE ISSUED AT 50% OVER THE THIRD CLASS FARE (fractions of a penny reckoned as a penny).

Passengers will be allowed to alight on the outward journey at a Station short of their destination on surrender of the outward half of their ticket, and on the return may commence their journey at an intermediate Station or complete it at a Station short of the destination shown on the ticket.

Children under three years of age, Free; three years and under fourteen, Half-fares.

CONDITIONS OF ISSUE OF EXCURSION TICKETS AND OTHER TICKETS AT LESS THAN ORDINARY FARE.

These Tickets are issued subject to the Notices and Conditions shown in the Company's Current Time Tables.

For LUGGAGE ALLOWANCES also see Time Tables.

PLEASE RETAIN THIS PROGRAMME FOR REFERENCE.

Further information may be obtained on application to any L M S Station or Office, or to J. A. MILLIGAN, District Passenger Manager, Euston Station, London, N.W.1.

January, 1935.   ASHTON DAVIES, Chief Commercial Manager.

M.R.O. 53360   50695—McCorquodale & Co., Ltd., London.

Above: LMS Cheap Ticket handbill for St Pancras and Bedford line, January 1935. *BR*

Below: LMS Third Class ticket, Harpenden-St Albans (City) with pull out advertising insertion, 1933. *Author*

Matthew Kirtley's condensing well-tanks, a design of engine which first appeared in 1868, could usually be seen acting as station pilots. It seemed in those days that these double-framed locomotives would last forever. At different times their numbers were 1211/3/4/6/9/20/2/5. Other venerable engines, which came as visitors, were 2-4-0s such as No 127 with 6ft 3in driving wheels, originally built in 1874 by Kirtley and rebuilt later by Johnson, and two of Johnson's own 2-4-0s with 6ft 9in driving wheels Nos 225/65 built between 1876-81. In the earlier part of the period Deeley's 'flat-iron' 0-6-4Ts such as Nos 2000/1/11 and Whitelegg LTS 4-6-4Ts Nos 2196/8 worked St Albans trains for a time.

Both stopping passenger trains and empty stock were hauled by another type of long lived engine — the Johnson 0-4-4Ts. Built between 1875 and 1900, the condensing versions worked on to the Metropolitan widened lines. Amongst those seen were Nos 1228/85/94/1309/12/3/5/7/20/1/43/71/3/4/6-85/9/1406/25/6/7. At various times I had runs behind about 15 of them, some of them quite frequently and visited the cab of No 1380. Another class much in evidence were the Johnson Class 3 4-4-0s, the original 'Belpaires', 80 of which had been built between 1900 and 1905. Good looking and hardworking with 6ft 9in driving wheels, they were mostly rebuilt by Fowler from 1913 onwards. They hauled a variety of trains and although unfortunately they never became an LMS standard, one at least lasted into the days of British Rail. As C. Hamilton Ellis wrote: 'They had been a very good investment'. It is interesting that the Fowler 2-6-4Ts used a superheated version of the same type of boiler. I saw many of the class and can recall Nos 701/7/8/10/5/9-21/3/5/6/33/50/3/5-760/2-5/7/8/774. I had runs behind some 13 of these engines on various occasions.

No Midland scene would be complete without the Johnson/Deeley 3-cylinder compound 4-4-0s and of the 16 I had runs behind at various times, two were rebuilds of the original Johnson engines Nos 2634/5, renumbered in 1907 Nos 1003/4. Of those seen there was No 1000 (now preserved), and Nos 1001/5/6/9-13/5-22/4/9/32-44. These were only the Compounds of Midland origin and of the 195 built by Fowler between 1924 and 1932, there were many present at St Pancras, such as Nos 1047-49/51/53-5/61/3/70/2/6/8/83/6/8/90/3/5/9/1188. No 1054 had appeared on the Midland division two years after its record breaking run (probably the longest in history for a 4-4-0), non-stop from Euston to Edinburgh on Friday, 27 April 1928 and was now attached to Kentish Town shed. It retained its tender, fitted with overhanging rails to increase its coal capacity to 9 tons. The last series of LMS Compounds built in 1932, Nos 925-8/31/3/5, also appeared. No 936, which I saw passing

Radlett, had the Stanier rebuild of a Fowler 3,500gal tender, with high curved sides. Numbered 3677, it had originally been attached to a '4F' 0-6-0.

Another type frequently observed at St Pancras was the Midland Class 2 4-4-0. These locomotives had originated with the Johnson small boilered engines, similar to those seen on the M&GN line, rebuilt by Deeley and then rebuilt by Fowler into virtually new engines. Never great on performance they were none the less robust and economical on repairs, useful for secondary duties. I rarely had a run behind one of these, but I saw a fair number of them such as Nos 337/404/10/11/6-8/20/1/2/5/6/37/62/93/9/500/ 15/35/9-45/9-62. The LMS version of which 138 were built between 1928 and 1932, appeared in my experience more often on other parts of the system, in fact I saw many of them on the former Glasgow & South Western, one of the Midland's Scottish partners.

Johnson Class 1 and 3 0-6-0Ts were often around the terminus, and of the former I recall Nos 1666/68/ 70-2/1713/21/4, the last two having open backed cabs. The Class 3s which formed the prototype for the Fowler LMS version were Nos 1902/8/15/19/20/2/4/ 8/40/5/6/7. With the exception of Johnson 0-6-0 No 3385, all the 0-6-0s I saw at the station were Fowler Class 4s. They were usually engaged on working passenger trains to Southend-on-Sea via Harringay Park and South Tottenham — a very old service, established long before the LTS became part of the Midland. 772 of the Fowler Class 4 0-6-0s were finally constructed, the first two prototypes being built at Derby in 1911, no more appearing until 1917. I saw No 3835, the earliest of the class, at St Pancras in 1933. When constructed this engine and No 3836 had engaged in comparative trials to determine the merits of the superheaters with which they were fitted, as against earlier saturated engines. No 3835 won the day. No 3964 was another Midland Class 4 that I noted, and of the LMS version the following Nos 4027/9/35/47/51/4082/4298/9/4403/18/26/29/ 4520/30/2/53.

In the first part of the 1930s the suburban duties of the Johnson 0-4-4Ts were being taken over by the Fowler LMS Class 3 2-6-2Ts Nos 15520-39 fitted with condensing apparatus and Weir feed pump. In 1934 they were renumbered Nos 21-40. I was hauled by every one of them, and one non-condensing version No 64. By 1935 a Stanier taper boiler development, No 90, first appeared in service. Both classes were undistinguished — not so the highly successful 2-6-4Ts design of both Fowler and Stanier (and looking into the future those of Fairburn and Riddles). In the late 1920s and the 1930s many of the fast runs out to Radlett, St Albans, Harpenden and Luton were in the care of the Fowler Class 4 2-6-4Ts of the 2300 series — over half of the first 25 of these were

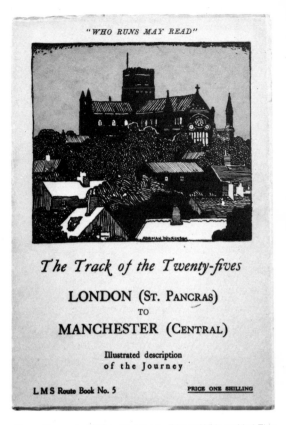

Above: Cover of a LMS publication by Edmund Vale entitled *The Track of the Twenty-fives,* an illustrated description of the journey over the Midland Division from London to Manchester. *BR*

originally painted in the LMS version of Midland red. No 2300 behind which I had many runs, at first appeared with smaller numerals on the bunker than the rest. The others I was hauled by were Nos 2301/2/ 22/5-9/35/6/50/3/74/80. The final batch appeared in 1933/34 under Stanier and had side window cabs, one of this type No 2400, I noted at Kentish Town.

These were followed in 1934 by the Stanier taper boiler 3-cylinder class which I saw under construction at Derby. The 37 locomotives were smooth running machines, and many of them appeared at St Pancras at one time or another. The one I never saw on the Midland, or its associated Southend line, was the prototype No 2500, which I first noted at Euston. During the second half of 1934 and the beginning of 1935, I had many runs behind them between Radlett

13

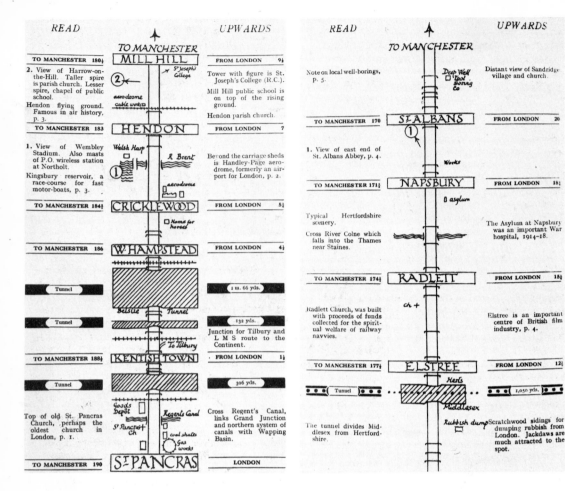

Above left: Page vii showing route map from St Pancras to Mill Hill. *BR*

Above: Page viii showing route map from Elstree to St Albans. *BR*

and St Pancras, the engines being Nos 2501/5/6/7/8/9/11/12/16. Although ultimately destined for the Southend line, I think that LTS destination board holders must have been fitted when they went to Plaistow, No 2501 certainly did not have them when I knew it.

As the 3-cylinder 2-6-4Ts gradually went to the LTS, the Fowler 2-6-4Ts reappeared, to be joined during 1936/7 by the Stanier 2-cylinder version. These engines also proved to be excellent performers and I noted Nos 2546/7/51, the last of which headed one of my Radlett trains.

Mostly observed in the neighbourhood of St Pancras or Kentish Town were the Horwich-designed 2-6-0 'Crabs', another type which performed well, and which had originally influenced the Fowler 2-6-4Ts. Those seen were Nos 2747/55/8-60/2/3/5/7/8/89-91/5/6/9/2826-29/36/7/9/45/6/70-4/6/95-9/2902-4.

Apart from the 2-6-0s and the occasional visit of a LNW 'Prince' or 'Claughton' (such as Nos 5757 and

5964 *Patriot* in its original form and the Fowler 5XP 'Patriot' rebuilds and their successors), six-coupled express motive power was in the care of the Stanier 2-cylinder Mixed Traffic 4-6-0s — known ever after as the 'Black Fives' — and the 3-cylinder 'Jubilee' 4-6-0s, successors to the 'Patriots'. It was about this time that Stanier must have suddenly become aware that some Swindon ideas did not necessarily meet the requirements of the more difficult conditions of the LMS. Indications that not all was well with the 'Jubilees'

14

became evident in various ways: I saw Nos 5606 and 5643 with front indicator shelters; No 5665 was seen with a dynamometer car in tow; and a number of engines appeared with altered chimneys. This was only external evidence that, amongst other things, the low superheat taper boilers did not steam as well as the normal superheat parallel boilers on the 'Patriots', from which the 'Jubilees' had been derived.

At first Stanier does not appear to have appreciated fully what had gone wrong. There followed a variety of experiments, some of which made matters worse, but finally the combination of an improved boiler with a 24-element superheater and reduced blast pipe solved the problem and they became excellent locomotives. But for a time it was a hard slog to make performance match appearance, for in their original condition they were attractive looking machines. One characteristic I did find, was that they appeared to fluctuate indiscriminately between the Midland and Western divisions, the engine seen at Euston one day, would be passing Radlett a week or so later. They may have been moved around in the search to find a solution to their problem. On the Midland during 1935, I was hauled by the following engines, Nos 5607/12/14/22/30/64, and noted at St Pancras and nearby Nos 5560/82/9/90/4/5/9/5606/7-38/40-43/6/9/52/5-67/71/2/80/7/5716/24/30. Some were named, but others had still to receive their plates.

The 'Black Fives' were luckier, for although better steaming they suffered to some degree from the same fault as the 'Jubilees'. However they proved so successful otherwise, that even before modification they began to build up a good reputation. At the time I had runs on the Division behind Nos 5056/65/7/90/5182, and noted Nos 5004/33-37/40-2/50/2-8/64/5/7-9/73/88-90/2/5115/9/53/4/78/80-2/84/5/7-90/3/5201/3/60/1/3/5-7/71/3/4/7-81/4-7/5316/35/77.

In the earlier part of the period there were the 'Twenty Fives', expresses to Manchester (Central) along the Midland route departing every two hours from St Pancras at 25 minutes past the hour. Scotland was served by the 'Thames-Clyde' and 'Thames-Forth' expresses for Glasgow (St Enoch) and Edinburgh (Waverley) respectively, over the old links with the Glasgow & South Western and North British railways.

In June, 1936, I returned to St Pancras from Glasgow on the 'Thames-Clyde' express. St Enoch station was the former headquarters of the GSWR, a line which for years had a close association with the Midland and shared Anglo-Scottish joint rolling stock. Its final Locomotive Superintendent at Kilmarnock had been Robert Whitelegg from the LTSR following its takeover by the Midland. At St Enoch, I was interested to see No 15405, one of his massive 4-6-4Ts. There were then only two left and I saw its companion, No 15404, at Ardrossan. These were of course developments of his design for the 'Tilbury'. Another GSW engine at St Enoch was No 14517, a Peter Drummond '325' class 4-4-0. I saw another member of the class at Ayr, No 14514, together with Drummond 0-6-2T No 16910.

The descendants of the Midland Compounds and Class 2 4-4-0s in their LMS form were much in evidence on the GSWR. Either at St Enoch or Ayr, I recall seeing Nos 912/5/6/1136/46/7 of the Compounds and Nos 573/4/9/92/641/4/7/669 of the Class 2s at St Enoch, and No 616 at Ayr.

From Glasgow my train was hauled by LMS Compound 4-4-0 No 1146 built in 1925, and Stanier 'Jubilee' 4-6-0 No 5622 *Nyasaland* as train engine. At Carlisle, where I noted another GSWR engine, Drummond 2-6-0 No 17825 of the '51' class built in 1915, the Compound came off the train and the 'Jubilee' continued south.

At St Pancras, in the midst of all the steam, there was a ripple of events to come, when at the end of the 1930s a 3-car LMS articulated diesel set appeared. This comprised cars Nos 80000/1/2 and was powered by six Leyland 125hp engines mounted under the floor, each driving a single axle via a torque converter. After experimental running on the Oxford and Cambridge branches, it entered regular passenger service on the Midland main line between St Pancras and Nottingham, covering some 350 miles daily. It was the first regular diesel train service from a London terminus.

On 20 March 1939, I travelled in this train from St Pancras to St Albans on what was probably one of these diagrams. The saloon carriages of the thirds had a light coloured decor, reversible seat backs and air operated doors. The exterior of the train had shaped ends with built in lights, and was painted bright red below the waist line and cream colour above, with a broad black band beneath the windows. The design of the articulation was used as the prototype for the LMS double-pivot system applied to the 1939 'Coronation Scot'. This LMS diesel set was an imaginative design. A recorded run between Nottingham and Kettering showed a lively performance with speeds in the 70s. If war had not come, the expereriment might have been repeated, as another set was marked on the construction diagram.

Some eight years later, diesel traction was to appear once again on the Midland division, when, in 1947, Derby completed the first main line diesel express locomotive, No 10000, to the overall design of the then LMS Chief Mechanical Engineer, H. G. Ivatt. Its first trials took place in 1948 under British Rail between St Pancras and Manchester and I was hauled by it on at least one occasion. The diesel age on Britain's railways was beginning.

Left: Sunshine and shadow under the great roof of St Pancras station (1948). *C. R. L. Coles*

Below: The lines into St Pancras with Somers Town goods station on right. *BR*

Above right: Kirtley, rebuilt Johnson, single framed 2-4-0 awaiting departure from St Pancras. No 127 was built in 1874. *Author*

Below right: Midland Class 2 4-4-0 No 557 of Kentish Town shed waiting to take over Tilbury boat train at St Pancras. *Author*

Above: Bedford-St Pancras fast train in the late-1920s hauled by Midland Class 2 4-4-0 No 559, rebuilt by Fowler in 1914.
F. R. Hebron/Rail Archive Stephenson

Right: The last of Midland construction, Class 2 4-4-0 No 562, rebuilt by Fowler in 1913. *Author*

18

Above: Originally known in Midland days as the 'Belpaires' and built by Johnson in 1900-5, mostly rebuilt by Fowler from 1913 onwards with superheaters. Class 3 4-4-0 No 758 awaits the 'off' on train at St Pancras. *Author*

Below: Up Bedford-St Pancras train with three Stanier carriages and LNW parcels vans hauled by Class 3 4-4-0 No 762 in 1937. *E. R. Wethersett/Ian Allan Library*

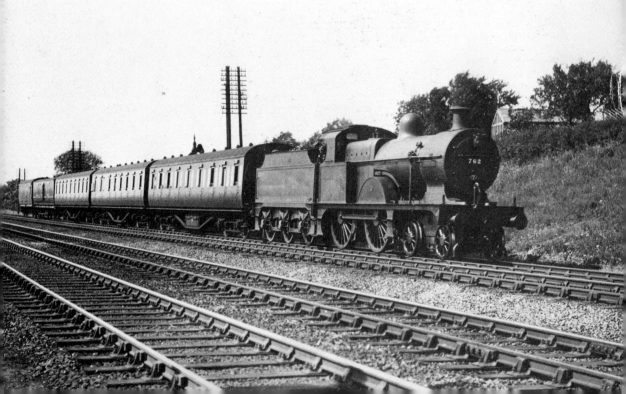

Top: Class 3 4-4-0 No 765 from Bedford shed on up train at St Albans City. Midland Clayton bogie clerestory with end luggage compartment next to engine. *Author*

Above: Deeley Class 4 3-cylinder Compound 4-4-0 No 1017, built 1906 and superheated 1926, on train about to leave St Pancras, until 1907 it was numbered 1012. *Author*

Above: Built in 1906 and superheated 1924, Deeley Class 4 3-cylinder Compound 4-4-0 No 1019 from Manchester shed at St Pancras. *Author*

Left: Fowler Class 4 Compound 4-4-0 No 1057 built by the LMS at Derby 1924, and from Derby shed, leaving arrival platform at St Pancras. This engine and No 1061 received Deeley long wheelbase tenders originally used by the '999' class 4-4-0s, with overhanging rails increasing capacity to 9 tons. One of these was used by No 6113, the 'Royal Scot' class 4-6-0 on its record breaking non-stop run to Glasgow on 27 April 1928, another Deeley long wheelbase tender being supplied to Compound 4-4-0 No 1054 which worked the Edinburgh non-stop record train. *Author*

Left: Under the great roof of St Pancras station, No 1071 of the 1924 series of LMS Compound 4-4-0s built at Derby. *Author*

Below: Night Scotch express leaving St Pancras with LMS Class 4 Compound 4-4-0 No 1097, built in 1925 at Derby.

Right: Another of the 1925 series built at Derby, LMS Class 4 Compound No 1107 backing out from arrival platform at St Pancras. *Author*

Below right: From the Midland to the Western division, LMS Class 4 Compound 4-4-0 No 1107 departing from Euston station. The same engine was noted at Derby in 1935, and at St Pancras. *Author*

Above: The last of the original Johnson Compounds, numbered 2635 until 1907, rebuilt by Deeley and renumbered 1004, superheated in 1914, on stopping train near Elstree in 1937. *E. R. Wethersett/IAL*

Below: Deeley Class 4 Compound 4-4-0 built 1906, No 1034 on down express near Elstree in 1930. *E. R. Wethersett/IAL*

Top: Compounds double-heading, leading engine No 1039 built 1908, of Kentish Town shed. *Author*

Above: Down St Pancras-Bradford express in 1935 near Mill Hill with Deeley Compound 4-4-0 No 1040 built 1909 and shedded at Leicester. *E. R. Wethersett/IAL*

Above: Double-heading on an up fast passing Elstree in 1937, LMS Compound No 1060 built Derby in 1924, piloted by Midland Class 2 4-4-0 No 559. *E. R. Wethersett/IAL*

Below: LMS Compound 4-4-0 No 1063 built 1924 on down fast at St Albans. *Author*

Above: Midland Class 2 0-6-0 No 3707 shunting at Elstree in 1937. Except for Deeley chimney and smokebox door, basically in original Johnson condition.
E. R. Wethersett/IAL

Left: LMS Compound 4-4-0 No 1146 built by North British Locomotive Co in 1925, as pilot on up 'Thames Clyde' express at St Enoch station, Glasgow, in 1936. *Author*

Top left: GSWR 4-6-4T No 15401 (541) built 1922 and designed by Robert Whitelegg formerly of the LTSR, on Ayr-St Enoch train about 1933.

Centre left: Peter Drummond GSWR 2-6-0 No 17830 (61) built 1915 on goods train.

Below: One of the original 'Baby Scots', later 'Patriot' class, rebuilt by Fowler in 1930 at Derby from LNWR 'Claughtons'. The large wheel centres and radial bogie of 3-cylinder 4-6-0 No 5971 indicate its origin. Departing Carlisle on the up 'Thames-Clyde' express in 1931.
F. R. Hebron/Rail Archive Stephenson

Right: Class 5XP 3-cylinder 4-6-0 No 5971 at Nottingham Midland.
T. G. Hepburn/Rail Archive Stephenson

Below right: St Pancras-Leeds express with milk tanks for Appleby in 1934 hauled by 5XP 3-cylinder 4-6-0 No 6011 *Illustrious*, built Crewe (termed rebuild) in 1933.
F. R. Hepburn/Rail Archive Stephenson

Top: Stanier 5XP 'Jubilee' class 4-6-0 No 5622 *Nyasaland*, built Crewe 1934, with domeless taper boiler as train engine on up 'Thames-Clyde' express at St Enoch station, Glasgow, in 1936. *Author*

Above: Departing St Pancras on down express circa 1936 Stanier 5XP 'Jubilee' 4-6-0 No 5656, later named *Cochrane*, and built Derby in 1935. *Author*

Above: Stanier 5XP 'Jubilee' 4-6-0 No 5664 *Nelson*, built Derby in 1935, on St Pancras-Kettering train in 1937. Original domeless boiler replaced by new version with separate dome and top feed. *E. R. Wethersett/IAL*

Below: Down St Pancras-Manchester express on the outskirts of St Albans hauled by 'Jubilee' 4-6-0 No 5682 *Trafalgar*, built Crewe 1936 with domed boiler, from Kentish Town shed. *E. D. Bruton*

Top: Stanier 'Black Five' 2-cylinder 4-6-0 No 5042 built by Vulcan Foundry about 1935 with domeless boiler, on down express near Elstree in 1937.   *E. R. Wethersett/IAL*

Above: Near Mill Hill in 1935 on down St Pancras-Bedford train, Stanier 'Black Five' No 5056 built by Vulcan Foundry with domeless boiler. On this and many other trains on the Division in the 1930s Midland clerestories were often in evidence.
E. R. Wethersett/IAL

Below: Hughes/Fowler mixed traffic 2-6-0 No 13203 built Crewe 1930, at St Pancras. *Author*

Bottom: Near Elstree in 1937, up Sheffield excursion hauled by Hughes/Fowler 2-6-0 No 2760 (formerly 13060) built Crewe in 1927. Until the coming of Stanier, these locomotives with their generally Lancashire & Yorkshire outline apart from the tenders represented the only radical departure from Derby practice, and had an influence on the Fowler 2-6-4Ts. It was due to the Midland loading gauge that the 'Crabs' as they became nicknamed received their steeply inclined cylinders. *E. R. Wethersett/IAL*

Above: A constant feature at St Pancras in the 1920s and early-1930s was the Kirtley 0-4-4 double-framed well tank on pilot duty. Built 1869-70 they were frequently to be seen pottering around the station, the last of the series, which originally comprised 26 engines, being scrapped in 1935. No 1208, one of the first batch at St Pancras in the early days of the LMS, in 1923 crimson-lake livery.
F. R. Hebron/Rail Archive Stephenson

Right: Johnson Class 1 0-4-4T No 1228, with heightened bunker rails, an early representative of a large class constructed between 1875 and 1900, and a mainstay on the Midland for suburban and local traffic.
Author

Above: Another view of Johnson Class 1 0-4-4T No 1228, which is virtually in original condition apart from chimney and smokebox door. The engine could be described as well coaled up. *Author*

Below: Johnson 0-4-4T No 1321 with condensing apparatus for working over the Metropolitan widened lines. At St Pancras on train of Express Dairy milk tanks from Cricklewood. *Author*

Left: Johnson condensing 0-4-4T No 1321 on pilot duty at St Pancras, Barlow's great roof soaring above, in the early 1930s. *Author*

Below: Many Johnson 0-4-4Ts were rebuilt from 1925 onwards with Belpaire fireboxes. No 1371 is an example of this. *Author*

Right: Another rebuilt Johnson 0-4-4T No 1373 in early 1930s. Both this engine and No 1371 were allocated BR numbers, in fact the last of the class was not withdrawn until 1960. *Author*

Below right: A condensing Johnson 0-4-4T in virtually original condition; No 1378 at Kentish Town. Deeley chimney and smokebox door. *Author*

Below: An earlier view, in 1926, of Johnson condensing 0-4-4T No 1321 in 1923 crimson-lake livery, and still retaining the original Johnson hand-rails, hauling a down Harpenden train near Mill Hill. Although the engine livery was to change to black, this scene with low arc roofed Midland suburban sets (which were quite comfortable), still remained common although Fowler 2-6-2Ts had taken over much of the work.
F. R. Hebron/Rail Archive Stephenson

Bottom: Down suburban near Elstree in 1931, hauled by Johnson 0-4-4T No 1375. By 1934 this particular locomotive had moved north and was attached to Derby shed.
H. C. Casserley

Above: Johnson Class 1 0-6-0T No 1721 with open back cab, rebuilt 1914, one of a series of 280 built between 1874 and 1900, many with full cabs. *Author*

Left: LMS President's Inspection Saloon at St Pancras in the early 1930s. Numbered 45000 and painted crimson lake with cream upper panels and two emblems each side, it was originally the LNWR Chairman's Saloon No 5000 and was built in 1920. It was later fitted with LMS bogies and finally by BR with bogies for 100mph running. *Author*

Bottom left: LNWR rolling stock on the Midland Division. Low arc roofed bogie corridor third No 4913, originally gas-lit and built between 1898 and 1903, and behind, elliptical roofed corridor carriage built sometime after 1908. *Author*

39

Above left: Fowler Class 3 2-6-2T No 15520 built Derby in 1930, one of the 20 fitted with condensing apparatus and Weir feed water pump, for use in the London area. Seen at St Albans, this engine became No 21 in the 1934 renumbering from 1-70 of the entire class. *Author*

Left: Fowler Class 3 2-6-2T No 15520, and the last of the first batch built Derby in 1930, on down suburban train near Mill Hill in 1931. *E. R. Wethersett/IAL*

Above: Belonging to Kentish Town shed, Fowler Class 3 2-6-2T No 15532 at St Pancras in early 1930s. *Author*

Left: Fowler Class 3 2-6-2T No 15532 renumbered 33 in 1934 entering Radlett station. Note the Midland inside keyed chairs on track near the buffer stop behind platform railing. *Author*

Below: Stanier taper boiler version of the Fowler 2-6-2T, No 90 built Derby 1935, when new on down St Albans train at Radlett. Stanier flush window steel panelled carriage. *Author*

Right: Leaving Elstree tunnel on down local in 1937, Stanier 2-6-2T No 90. Later members of the class had a domed boiler with separate top feed. *E. R. Wethersett/IAL*

Below right: Deeley Class 3 0-6-4T No 2013 built 1907 and rebuilt by Fowler with Belpaire firebox and superheater, departing from St Pancras for St Albans with train of Midland Bain wide bodied suburban stock in 1926. Several of these locomotives worked in the London area including Nos 2000/1. *F. R. Hebron/Rail Archive Stephenson*

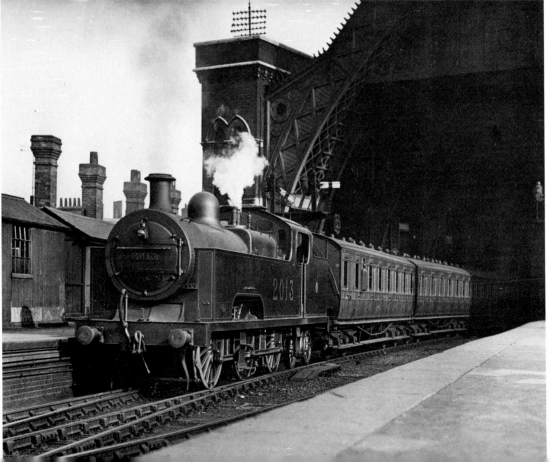

Above left: The first of the Fowler Class 4 2-6-4Ts No 2300, built at Derby in 1927 in the crimson lake livery carried by the earlier members of the class (No 2300 was the only one to have small numerals), on up St Pancras train at St Albans. Deeley originally considered this wheel arrangement when he designed his 0-6-4Ts. The Fowler engines could be said to have descended from them, but influenced by the Horwich designed LMS 2-6-0s. They proved to be one of Fowler's most successful locomotives. *LPC*

Left: Fowler Class 4 2-6-4T No 2300 on down local near Elstree in 1931. *H. Gordon Tidey*

Above: Fowler Class 4 2-6-4T No 2327 built Derby 1929, ready to leave St Pancras for St Albans. End of leading coach has oval enamelled plate showing weight, introduced by the Midland in 1907. *Author*

Bottom: Fowler 2-6-4T No 2328 on down local near Elstree in 1930.
F. R. Wethersett/IAL

Below: Near Elstree in 1931, up train including Clayton and Bain bogie clerestories hauled by Fowler 2-6-4T No 2328 built at Derby in 1929. *H. C. Casserley*

Top: The second of the 3-cylinder Stanier Class 4 2-6-4Ts No 2501 built Derby in 1934, at Radlett when new. Although ultimately intended for the Southend line, quite a number of these well thought of engines spent considerable time in their earlier days on the St Pancras, St Albans and Luton main line. Among those operating in 1934-5 were Nos 2501/5/6/7/8/9/11/16. It will be noted that when new No 2501 was not fitted with destination board holders, which must have been fitted later at Plaistow. *Author*

Above: LMS 3-car articulated diesel train built 1938 about to leave St Pancras on inaugural day of main line service in 1939. Fowler condensing 2-6-2T No 21, built Derby 1930, alongside. *Railway Magazine*

Below: LMS 3-car articulated diesel train, numbered 80000/1/2, exterior painted red below and cream above, divided by a black band, with LMS emblem painted midway between waist band and cantrail on each unit. The roof is thought to have been a silver colour. The train was driven by six Leyland 125hp engines, two mounted under the floor of each car, each driving a single axle via a torque converter. The articulation was to the LMS system using a double pivot, and was used as the prototype for the 1939 'Coronation Scot' train. Like the latter the body side panels were taken right down between the bogies, but these were soon cut back. The end cars were divided into two saloons seating in total 54 third class passengers, most of the seats being reversible. There was a small lavatory in each car and a luggage and brake compartment. Access to each vehicle was by means of air operated sliding doors in the centre. The driving cabs were spacious and the driver centrally placed. The centre car was a composite with two saloons separated by an entrance vestibule. The third class saloon seated 30 passengers with luggage racks and a lavatory, the seats being reversible. The first class saloon seated 24 passengers in varied fashion, but throughout the train all seats were placed in pairs either side of a centre gangway. The seating was comfortable and the design of the train imaginative. If war had not come another set would probably have been built, as it was marked on the diagram. *Crown Copyright, National Railway Museum, York*

Bottom: At Luton station LMS articulated diesel train on down St Pancras-Nottingham service in late 1939. *W. S. Garth*

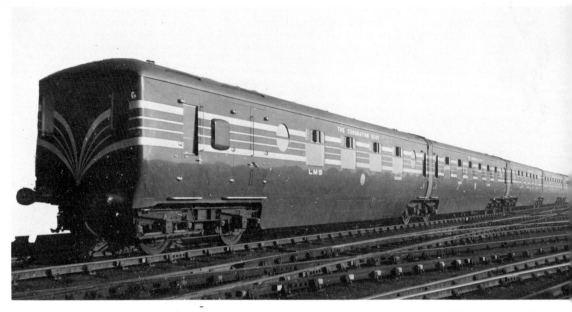

Above: 1939 'Coronation Scot' set showing articulated bogie, first tried out on the diesel set.
Crown Copyright, National Railway Museum, York

Below: Completed after the war by the LMS at Derby in 1947, Ivatt's diesel-electric Co-Co express locomotive No 10000 leaving Luton on a Manchester-St Pancras express. Livery was black with an aluminium trim. *W. S. Garth*

Sheds Along the Line

When the Midland built its London extension to the magnificent new terminus at St Pancras, it was essential that operation of the new line maintained an equally high standard. To help to meet this goal, the locomotive shed at Kentish Town was regarded for years as one of the most important on the railway. By the 1890s this had been emphasised by the appointment of Robert Weatherburn as London District Locomotive Superintendent.

Son of the driver of the *Comet* on the Leicester & Swannington, he had worked for Kitson & Co of Leeds, where he had been concerned with delivery of engines constructed by that firm to Kirtley's designs for the Midland. In an article he later wrote for the *Railway Magazine* he paid this tribute to Kirtley's engines: 'They did the work for which they were designed excellently, and nothing that came after them gave better results in proportion to size and steam pressure.'

It will be seen by this that Weatherburn was not a man afraid to express his opinions and he was also not backward in taking the initiative when required. After joining the Midland, he became District Locomotive Superintendent at Leicester in 1884. Due to the experiments he carried out while in that post with an old disused single driver, proving that adhesion problems could be overcome by placing adequate sanding under the 'spinners', he reawakened Johnson's interest in the type. Following the invention of steam sanding by another Midland man, Francis Holt, the development of Johnson's shapely 4-2-2s was assured. It should also be mentioned that Weatherburn suggested to Johnson the use of a leading bogie. The latter was reluctant to take up new ideas until they were proven (we can appreciate the virtue of this even better today), but he was always prepared to listen.

As far back as 1875, Weatherburn had also expounded to Johnson on the virtues of the Belpaire firebox, but it was not until 1900 that the latter produced the 4-4-0s known as the Belpaires, the '700' class in the Deeley renumbering, which proved of so much value to the Midland. They were closely followed by the Belpaire 4-4-0 Compounds. Johnson always the gentleman, later recalled Weatherburn's early suggestion.

It will be seen that Kentish Town shed was in the

charge of a trusted Johnson man of considerable ability and drive. Needless to say, Kentish Town's non-failure record became an example to the whole system. It also had its own paint shop, as did Manchester, Leeds and some other major depots, and something like a London school of painting developed under Weatherburn, with certain embellishments — a deepening of the crimson lake and cream lining instead of yellow. Kentish Town became a shed with a personality.

Sheds were numbered outwards from Derby by the Midland and the allocation of '16' on some locomotives lasted well into LMS days, even though by that time the shed had been renumbered 14B. In addition to main line activities, it provided motive power for the East Ham, Barking and Metropolitan widened line services. Not inappropriately for a system which had one of its roots in Burton-on-Trent, a baronial turretted brewery bottling stores ran down one side and provided a popular background for photographing locomotives over the years.

I first went there in 1934 and saw Kirtley 0-4-4WT No 1222, Johnson condensing 0-4-4Ts Nos 1371/80, Johnson Class 1 0-6-0Ts Nos 1661/71/1713/91, Class 3 0-6-0Ts Nos 1905/20/7/9/41/2/4 and Fowler 0-6-0Ts Nos 7102/3, LTSR Whitelegg 4-6-4T No 2198 which was possibly at that time still working the occasional St Albans train, Midland Class 2 4-4-0s Nos 539/54/56-59 and 561, Class 3 4-4-0 No 720, Deeley Class 4 4-4-0 Compounds Nos 1013/6/21/35/6/9/43 and LMS Fowler Compound No 925 of the very last series built in 1932. There was also one 'Patriot' 4-6-0 No 5958.

A longer visit in 1936 produced a more detailed record, with the additional interest of Divisional Engineer's Inspection saloon No 45032. Formerly a West Coast Joint clerestory 45ft 0in family saloon, LNW No 354, it was originally built at Wolverton in 1899. A long lasting vehicle it was to be seen some 10 years later behind Midland Class 2 4-4-0 No 548 at Upminster on inspection duty. Among the array of engines on shed in March 1936 were 'Jubilee' 4-6-0s Nos 5614/32/5 (from Derby), 5649 (from Sheffield), 5657 (from Nottingham), 5663/4; Class 5 ('Black Five') 4-6-0s Nos 5054/5/8/88 (from Millhouses); Hughes 2-6-0s Nos 2753/84 (both from Leeds), 2795/2826 (from Nottingham) 2870 (which I was to see later in the year at Glasgow Central), 2872; LMS Compound Class 4 4-4-0 No 1086 (from Leeds), Midland Class 3 4-4-0 No 720 (stored); Class 2 4-4-0s Nos 545 (from Leicester) 555/6/7/9/61; LMS Class 2 4-4-0 No 600; Johnson 0-4-4Ts Nos 1315/71/4/6/8/9/80/5/1406; Class 1 0-6-0Ts Nos 1660/1/4/6/8/71/2/1713/91; Class 3 0-6-0Ts Nos 1900 (from St Albans), 1941 (later seen at Cannon St SR) 1904/6/7/9/7206 (from Cricklewood) 7228/9/40/2/5 (both the

Johnson and Fowler engines were in process of being renumbered); Fowler Class 3 0-6-0Ts Nos 7103/7427/9/7514/7538/16514/16723; Johnson 0-6-0s Nos 3385/3517/3800; Fowler Class 4 0-6-0s Nos 4002/23 (from Belle Vue), 4050/1/2/4234/50/4531; Fowler 2-6-4Ts Nos 2326/80 (from St Albans); Stanier 3-cylinder 2-6-4T No 2528 (from Shoeburyness); Fowler 2-6-2T No 28, and LNW Whale Class G 0-8-0 No 9108 (1687).

Cricklewood shed No 15 (LMS 14A) was originally named Childs Hill. An important depot for freight and mineral traffic operation, its history over the years had been inescapably linked with Toton, located just below the southern edge of the Nottingham and Derbyshire coalfield, on the Chesterfield, Trent (Erewash Valley) main line. Toton yard extending for some $1\frac{1}{2}$ miles was an important 'pit head' for coal supplies to the rest of the country and especially London. The heavy coal trains up to the metropolis were a source of much double heading by the Midland and in the early LMS era. For many years the small engine policy then in fashion, involved the use of 0-6-0s in tandem. Henry Fowler did experiment with his 2-8-0s designed for the Somerset & Dorset, but there were clearance problems and troubles with the bearings over the long haul. The 0-10-0 Lickey banker was tried without success, LTS Whitelegg 4-6-4Ts sometimes with a 2-4-0 or a Johnson 'single' as pilot were used for a time, the latter a most unlikely choice. Fowler's Class 7 0-8-0s were also tried, but it was the Beyer-Garratt 2-6-0+0-6-2s which finally cut out most of the double heading. Later the Stanier 2-8-0s played their part in this heavy continuous traffic.

I first went to Cricklewood shed towards the latter end of 1934 and recall Johnson 0-6-0s Nos 3177/3256/3313/47/52/84/3554/65/3772/3813; Fowler Class 4 0-6-0s Nos 3910/9/35/65/4028/4228/4531; Johnson Class 1 0-6-0Ts Nos 1668/1710/2/4/80/1811/29/54; Johnson Class 3 0-6-0Ts fitted with condensing apparatus, Nos 1900-2/7-12/21/22/24/26/28; Fowler Class 3 0-6-0Ts Nos 16515/16/17/22; and Deeley Class 4 Compound 4-4-0s Nos 1008/19.

Engines noted in 1935 were Johnson 0-6-0 No 3270, Fowler Class 4 0-6-0s Nos 4107/4298, Fowler 0-8-0s Nos 9589/9624/30, Beyer Peacock Garratt 2-6-0+0-6-2s Nos 4984-87/9/91/5-7, Hughes 2-6-0s Nos 2753/2870. The first hundred of these Moguls were painted in crimson lake livery and No 2753 was still in this finish at the shed with its original pre-1934 number of 13053, its new number written below the emblem on the cab side. I later saw the same engine painted black.

In 1936 I saw two rare visitors, Johnson 6ft 9in 2-4-0 No 242 at Cricklewood and, passing through Somerset & Dorset 4-4-0 No 78, renumbered in LMS stock as Class 2 No 321. This was one of the two

4-4-0s possessing straight footplates built by Deeley in 1908 and rebuilt with Belpaire firebox in 1921. Other engines noted were Hughes 2-6-0s Nos 2897/2900/3/28, Stanier 2-8-0s Nos 8003/10/35/47/9/50/1, Johnson 0-6-0s Nos 3508/17, Fowler 0-8-0 No 9596 of the original 1929 batch and Beyer Peacock Garratt 2-6-0+0-6-2s Nos 4977/83/94.

Between Cricklewood and Elstree on the south side of Elstree tunnel are Scratchwood sidings, a great haunt for jackdaws as it was the place that rubbish from London was dumped. Hughes 2-6-0s often worked there and I recall seeing Nos 2747/71/74/97/2827/30/71, so it would seem this was a regular roster for these engines.

Bedford shed No 14 (LMS 15D) served, in addition to the main line, branches to Northampton and Hitchin. The latter was the legacy from the days before the London extension was built, when Kirtley 2-4-0s would work expresses from Leicester via Bedford and Hitchin to Kings Cross. Years later when the Midland presence at the GNR London terminus had become long forgotten, the LMS still showed in its Bedford and Hitchin timetable, connections with Leicester and Kings Cross, thus maintaining in spirit the ancient link. Not only that, Bedford station itself remained orientated towards Hitchin instead of St Pancras and this has only recently been rectified with the new station built in connection with the BR electrification.

Like Wellingboro' and Kettering further north, Bedford was a home for 2-4-0s. When I was at the shed in 1934, there was one Kirtley 6ft 8½in single framed locomotive, No 115, which had been rebuilt by Johnson, his own 6ft 6in 2-4-0s Nos 179/88 and 6ft 9in engines Nos 228/67. Other Johnson locomotives were 0-4-4Ts Nos 1239/60/72/3/1369, Class 2 '483' rebuild 4-4-0 No 553, Class 3 4-4-0s Nos 719/753/6/59/60/5/7 and 0-6-0s Nos 2976/3119/3477/3609/3707/11/3805. Another 2-4-0 I saw at Bedford although I have no date, was Kirtley's 6ft 8½in single framed No 70, rebuilt by Johnson. In July 1936 I had a run behind No 267 mentioned above, from Bedford through Olney to Northampton.

Wellingboro' shed No 13 (LMS 15A) also served a link with Northampton. This was the line through Castle Ashley and Billing, the Midland having secured running powers over the LNW in 1850. The other line from Wellingboro' ran through Rushden to Higham Ferrers. So two branches were involved, apart from the main line.

The shed, another home for 2-4-0s, had an interesting occupant in 1934, Kirtley 6ft 3in double framed 2-4-0 No 12, but bearing a Kettering Plate. Earlier I had seen this engine in a siding near Chesterfield in company with Kirtley double-framed 0-6-0 No 2631. A companion engine to No 12 is No 2,

now preserved in Midland pre-1907 livery as No 158A. Another 2-4-0, but officially shedded at Wellingboro' was Johnson No 194 with 6ft 9in driving wheels. Other Johnson locomotives seen were Class 3 4-4-0s Nos 739/63, Class 4 Compound 4-4-0 No 1004, the last of the original engines Johnson Nos 2631-5, built in 1903, rebuilt by Deeley, and then by Fowler in 1914 to conform with the Deeley design of 1905. The first of this group of rebuilds has been preserved as No 1000. Another Johnson locomotive was Somerset & Dorset 0-4-4T No 52, renumbered into the LMS in 1930 as 1230. Other engines noted were Johnson Class 1 0-6-0T No 1660 and Fowler Class 3 No 16520, Johnson 0-6-0s Nos 3040/3113/3709/77/96/7/3806/13/14/29, Midland Fowler 0-6-0s Nos 3901/37/63/6/77/ and their LMS successors Nos 4230/1/5/79.

Kettering shed No 12 (LMS 15B), north of which the Midland main line to Leicester, Sheffield, Leeds and Scotland divided to Nottingham, dividing yet again at Trent to go north-westwards to Derby and Manchester. South-east from Kettering was the Midland's link with Cambridge through Thrapston to Huntingdon, where Derby had originally secured running powers over the Great Eastern into the university town. It was at Cambridge that I went in the cab of Johnson 6ft 9in 2-4-0 No 222, which was on this service.

At Kettering in 1934, I recall there were Johnson 6ft 9in 2-4-0s Nos 253/66, Class 2 4-4-0s Nos 424/5/6, 0-6-0s Nos 2930/63/7/8 with 4ft 11in wheels, No 3042 with 5ft 3in wheels, No 3139 with 4ft 11in wheels, Nos 3195/9/3333/3481/3545/64/6/3601/3781/2/2832 and Fowler Class 4s Nos 3949/3951 all with 5ft 3in wheels. Johnson 0-6-0 No 3333 was one of three given 6ft 0in driving wheels in 1906, its pre-1907 number was 2056. In the rebuilding Deeley provided these engines with new frames, and they were tried out on semi-fast passenger work. No 3333 reverted to 5ft 3in wheels in 1924.

Further north I made some random observations between 1934-6. At Leicester there were Deeley 0-6-4T No 2037, Midland Class 2 4-4-0s Nos 535/6/9/50/8, Class 4 Compound 4-4-0 No 1044, originally built in 1909 the last of Midland Construction, Fowler 2-6-4T No 2331, Stanier 'Black Five' 4-6-0 No 5187, Midland 0-6-0s Nos 3419/3467, LMS Class 4 No 4163 and LTS 4-2-2T No 2093. At Birmingham, I recall three Deeley 0-6-4Ts, Nos 2015 (which I saw later in Derby erecting shop) 2023/4 and at Trent No 2002, Johnson 0-4-4T No 1327, LMS 0-4-4T No 6403. At Sheffield Johnson 0-4-4Ts Nos 1238/1368, Midland Class 2 4-4-0 No 516, Hughes 2-6-0 No 2828, whilst at Leeds there were Johnson 0-4-4Ts Nos 1296/1353/1401/2, Midland Class 2 4-4-0s 479/80 and Fowler 2-6-4T No 2337.

Above: Kirtley Class 1 double framed 2-4-0 No 3 at Kentish Town in 1926. *F. R. Hebron/Rail Archive Stephenson*

Below: Kirtley condensing 0-4-4WT No 1219 at Kentish Town coaling stage. *Author*

Top: Johnson Class 3 0-6-0T, rebuilt with Belpaire firebox, new cab, Deeley chimney and smokebox door, No 1915 with condensing apparatus, at Kentish Town. *Author*

Above: The Fowler development of the Johnson engine, Class 3 0-6-0T at Kentish Town, No 16512, built by Hunslet in 1926. *T. G. Hepburn/Rail Archive Stephenson*

Above: Deeley 3-cylinder Compound 4-4-0 No 1013 (pre-1907 No 1008), built Derby 1905, at Kentish Town shed in 1934. *Author*

Below: LMS Fowler 3-cylinder Compound 4-4-0 No 1072, built Derby 1924 at Kentish Town in 1933 after repair following the Ambergate accident. *E. R. Wethersett/IAL*

Below: Hughes/Fowler 2-6-0 No 13174, built at Crewe in 1930, at Kentish Town in front of the brewery bottling store. *LPC*

Bottom: London & North Western Railway. 'Claughton' 4-cylinder 4-6-0 No 5974 (1747) with ROD tender at Kentish Town. *H. C. Casserley*

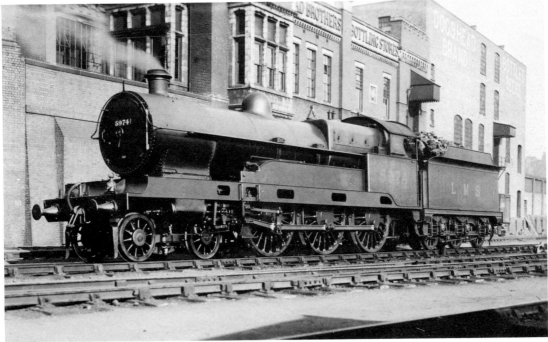

Below: One of the first two nominal rebuilds at Derby in 1930 from 4-cylinder LNWR 'Claughton' into 3-cylinder Class 5XP 'Baby Scot' (later termed 'Patriot' class), No 5902 renumbered in 1934 as 5501, and original LNW name of *Sir Frank Ree*. At Kentish Town; the 'Claughton' wheels can clearly be seen. *H. C. Casserley*

Bottom: Class 5XP 4-6-0 No 5933, a Derby 'rebuild' of 1933, at Kentish Town shed in 1934. *E. R. Wethersett/IAL*

Above: A nominal 'rebuild' of Crewe in 1932, Class 5XP No 5958 at Kentish Town shed. These speedy engines led the way to the 'Jubilees'. *Author*

Below: Another 'Baby Scot' Class 5XP No 5963 a nominal 'rebuild' of Derby in 1933, at Kentish Town shed. The final series of these locomotives were officially termed 'new' engines, which the majority had been all along anyway. *H. C. Casserley*

Above: Divisional Engineer's Inspection saloon No 45032 located at Kentish Town. Formerly West Coast Joint stock No 354, with clerestory roof. *Author*

Below: Fowler LMS Class 3 0-6-0T No 16516, built Hunslet 1926, and its forerunner Johnson Class 3 condensing 0-6-0T No 1909 built between 1899 and 1902, with original Johnson cab and fittings apart from Deeley chimney and smokebox door, at Cricklewood shed in 1934. *Author*

Top: Johnson Class 3 0-6-0T No 1917 rebuilt by Fowler with Belpaire boiler and new cab, at Cricklewood in 1934.
E. R. Wethersett/IAL

Above: Hughes/Fowler Class 4 (later Class 5) 2-6-0 No 13145 built Horwich 1930, at Cricklewood in 1931.
E. R. Wethersett/IAL

Left: In 1907, Deeley built at Derby, two 4-4-0s for the Somerset & Dorset Joint Railway Nos 77 and 78. These were rebuilt with Belpaire fireboxes in 1921, and taken into LMS stock in 1930. They were Class 2 and received the numbers 320 and 321. No 321 was seen working in the early 1930s on the Midland Division main line at Cricklewood, and the photograph shows its companion in S&D colours as No 77 at Bath in 1929. *H. C. Casserley*

Bottom left: Midland Class 3 4-4-0 No 759 superheated by Fowler in 1923 at Cricklewood in 1934. *E. R. Wethersett/IAL*

Below: Midland Class 3 0-6-0 No 3256 at Cricklewood, reboilered from a Johnson Class 2. *Author*

Bottom: One of the final batch of Class 4 0-6-0s to Fowler design, No 4529 built at Crewe in 1928. *Author*

Top: LMS Fowler Class 7 0-8-0 No 9630 built at Crewe in 1931, from Toton shed, at Cricklewood in 1935. *Author*

Above: Up heavy coal train leaving Nottingham with two Midland Class 3 0-6-0s, No 3763 leading.
T. G. Hepburn/Rail Archive Stephenson

Top right: Hughes/Fowler 2-6-0 No 2870 (pre-1934 No 13170) built Crewe 1930, on up coal train passing Elstree in 1937.
E. R. Wethersett/IAL

Centre right: Fowler Class 7 0-8-0 No 9504, one of the first batch of these engines built in 1929, on up Toton coal train coming out of Nottingham.
T. G. Hepburn/Rail Archive Stephenson

Bottom right: Passing Elstree in 1937, Stanier Class 8 2-8-0 No 8048 built Vulcan Foundry about 1937, on up coal train.
E. R. Wethersett/IAL

Above: Stanier Class 8 2-8-0 No 8069, built Vulcan Foundry about 1937, leaving Nottingham on Melton Mowbray line with up coal train in 1938. *T. G. Hepburn/Rail Archive Stephenson*

Below: Beyer-Garratt 2-6-0+0-6-2 on up coal train passing Elstree in 1937. Fitted with rotating coal bunker. *C. R. L. Coles*

Above: One of the second batch of Beyer-Garratt 2-6-0+0-6-2s, No 4994 built 1930 with improved coal bunker and heightened chimney. Fitted with rotating coal bunker in 1933. On down empty wagon train north of Elstree.
F. R. Hebron/Rail Archive Stephenson

Left: Johnson 2-4-0 No 179 of the class built between 1876-80, at Bedford shed in 1934, mostly in original condition. *Author*

Above: Rebuilt by Fowler with Belpaire firebox, Johnson 2-4-0 No 20251 (pre-1934 No 251) of the series built 1876-1881, at Bedford station in 1939.
C. R. L. Coles

Left: Johnson 0-4-4T No 1273 on Northampton-Bedford train in 1939.
H. C. Casserley

Above: Midland Class 2 4-4-0 No 552 with ash ejector at Wellingborough shed in 1934. *Author*

Below: Beyer-Garratt 2-6-0+0-6-2 No 4993 fitted with 10ton capacity rotating bunker, at Wellingborough shed. *T. G. Hepburn/Rail Archive Stephenson*

Top: Johnson Class 2 0-6-0 No 3042, rebuilt with Belpaire boiler and Deeley cab and Johnson 2-4-0 No 20216 (pre-1934 No 216) of the series built 1876-1881, rebuilt with Belpaire firebox, at Kettering in 1939. *C. R. L. Coles*

Above: Kirtley double framed 2-4-0 No 20012 (pre-1934 No 12) of the series built 1866-74, in rebuilt condition on a Cambridge-Kettering train near Cranford in 1937. A member of this class is preserved in original Midland livery as No 158A. *T. G. Hepburn/Rail Archive Stephenson*

Above: Johnson 2-4-0 No 207 on Kettering-Cambridge train in 1934. *E. R. Wethersett/IAL*

Below: At Cambridge LNER (Great Eastern) in mid-1930s, Kirtley 2-4-0 No 107, single framed rebuilt Johnson, of the series built 1871-75 on Kettering train. *A. H. Blake/IAL*

Right: Johnson Class 1 2-4-0 No 222 of the series built 1876-81 at Cambridge LNER (Great Eastern) on Kettering train. Great Eastern clerestory bogie carriage built about 1901 in background. *Author*

Below: Johnson Class 2 0-6-0 No 22930 (pre-1934 No 2930), rebuilt with Belpaire firebox and Deeley cab, on train from Cambridge approaching Kettering in 1939. *C. R. L. Coles*

Above: Kettering-Nottingham local train near Grendon North junction in 1939 hauled by Johnson 2-4-0 No 20251 (pre-1934 No 251). Rebuilt with Belpaire firebox.
C. R. L. Coles

Left: Class 3 4-4-0 No 762 of Kettering shed on train approaching Kettering in 1939, LNWR corridor carriage in background. *C. R. L. Coles*

Above: Class 3 4-4-0 No 712
on a 'special' at Bristol
Temple Meads in 1937.
C. R. L. Coles

Right: Class 2 4-4-2T
No 2101 (formerly LTSR
No 60 *Highgate*) from
Mansfield shed at Nottingham
in 1937. *H. C. Casserley*

Iron Horses at Derby

In 1844, the North Midland, Midland Counties and Birmingham & Derby Junction Railways amalgamated to form the Midland Railway Company, Derby becoming the headquarters of the largest railway in England at that time under one management. Matthew Kirtley of the Birmingham & Derby Junction, the smallest of these concerns, became the Locomotive & Carriage Superintendent of the new company, probably on the recommendation of George and Robert Stephenson. It proved to be an excellent choice and provided the Midland and its successor the LMS with sturdy reliable locomotives, some of which had an extraordinary life span.

Kirtley died in 1873 and was succeeded at Derby by Samuel Johnson, who came from the Great Eastern. The robust qualities of Kirtley were followed by a more genteel approach — fitness for purpose included appearance. Kirtley laid the foundations of the Derby tradition, Johnson developed and refined it into an art.

Shortly before Kirtley's death it had been decided to separate the growing carriage and wagon section from the locomotive side, and Thomas Clayton was appointed to the new department. This proved to be another sound choice and paved the way for that other Midland tradition inherited by the LMS — passenger comfort. In 1902, Clayton was succeeded by David Bain from the North Eastern, a line whose carriage design policy had much in common with Derby.

Richard Deeley took office as Locomotive Superintendent in 1904 and embarked on a massive reorganisation of Derby works. He introduced the drastic renumbering of 1907 where engines were grouped according to type, with power classification and smokebox numberplates — features which lasted through LMS days, as did his characteristic outline.

Unfortunately, Deeley became involved in one of those power struggles possibly exacerbated by his own personality, which occasionally arise in large organisations. His works manager at Derby was Cecil Paget, an inventive engineer and, into the bargain, son of the Chairman of the company. In 1907 Paget was promoted to the post of General Superintendent, a rank which brought him above Deeley, and Henry Fowler moved up to be Works Manager, Fowler and James Anderson, the Chief Locomotive Draughtsman were to be very important names for the rest of the Midland history, and well into the earlier period of the LMS.

Both Deeley and Paget had interesting ideas for larger and more powerful engines for the Midland, and if the former's conception of a 3-cylinder Compound 4-6-0 had not been thwarted by the revolutionary experimental rotary valve 2-6-2 locomotive No 2299, initiated and mainly paid for by Paget, the Midland and LMS's early small engine policy might have been considerably modified. Equally, the same result might have been attained if Paget's advanced brain child, completed in 1909, had been allowed to overcome its valve troubles. Unfortunately information regarding this engine is very scanty, but it is reported to have worked a test train between Derby and London, and Manchester reaching the unconfirmed speed of over 80mph.

Breaking point came for Deeley when it was decided to split the post of Locomotive Superintendent into two appointments, Chief Mechanical Engineer and Chief Motive Power Superintendent, a move which by dividing the power base was eventually to perpetuate the small engine policy already mentioned. Richard Deeley was 'incensed' by the move and tendered his resignation in 1909 to leave locomotive design for ever.

The stage was now set for Henry Fowler to be promoted to the new post. An organisation man, he is reputed to have said in a light moment that he never designed a locomotive in his life. To the extent that most locomotive engineers depend on their design team and especially their locomotive draughtsmen, this could be said to hold a grain of truth. In any case new construction between 1910 and 1917 was very thin on the ground at Derby, although the Fowler Class 4F 0-6-0, introduced in 1911, was to be built for the next 31 years and reach over 700 in number.

However, on the staff at Derby was someone who did have considerable influence on design. James Clayton, who had been associated with Sir Cecil Paget, as he became, in the design of the 2-6-2, undeniably left his mark on British locomotive design. Having served his time with Beyer, Peacock & Co Ltd,

Midland Railway, Rails and Chairs used from 1850 to 1897

Mechanical Engineers 1898.

he had joined the South Eastern & Chatham Railway as a draughtsman under Robert Surtees, who had been responsible for the design of the details of Wainwright's locomotives. Leaving the SECR in 1903, he became associated with the Paget experiment being provided with a small office near Derby station. He then went on to join the Midland Railway staff in 1905 and between 1907 and 1914 was one of the two chief assistants to James Anderson in the locomotive drawing office at Derby. Among locomotives for which he was largely responsible were the Somerset & Dorset Fowler 2-8-0s. To his chagrin, when the post of Chief Draughtsman came to be filled in 1913, he was passed over in favour of S. J. Symes, Anderson's other deputy. In that same year, R. E. L. Maunsell of the Great Southern & Western Railway of Ireland had been appointed Chief Mechanical Engineer to the South Eastern & Chatham and began to collect a team around him. It was not long before Clayton rejoined his old line as Chief Locomotive Draughtsman, becoming in 1919 Maunsell's personal assistant — a position he was to hold through to Southern Railway days. On the last absence of Maunsell through ill-health, Clayton became Acting Chief Mechanical Engineer to the Southern.

In 1923 the Midland became part of the London, Midland & Scottish Railway, the largest of the four

Above: Midland Railway rails and chairs used from 1850 to 1897, an engraving from Samuel Johnson's Presidential address of 1898 to the Institution of Mechanical Engineers. *Institution of Mechanical Engineers*

Above right: Passenger vehicles of the Midland Railway and its ancestors between 1839 and 1874 from Samuel Johnson's Presidential Address of 1898. *Institution of Mechanical Engineers*

Right: Midland passenger vehicles of Thames Clayton, 1875 to 1897, an engraving from Samuel Johnson's 1898 Presidential Address. *Institution of Mechanical Engineers*

groups, which meant that Derby was now in competition with Crewe and Horwich. The new Chief Mechanical Engineer was George Hughes from the Lancashire & Yorkshire Railway with the by now Sir Henry Fowler as Assistant CME. James Anderson, the believer in a small engine policy was now Chief Motive Power Superintendent, and in a powerful position. It was almost as though history was repeating itself.

George Hughes retired in 1925 having as his memorial the excellent 2-6-0 'Crabs', which did not appear until after he had gone, and Sir Henry Fowler

Plate 32.

PRESIDENT'S ADDRESS.

Midland Passenger Vehicles. 1839 to 1874.

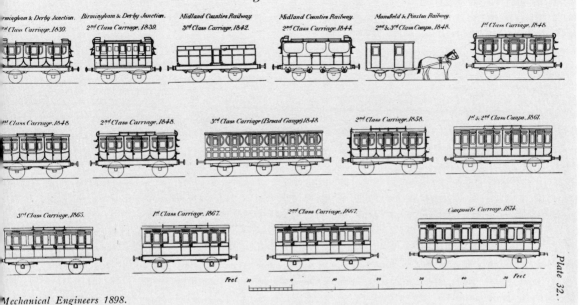

Birmingham & Derby Junction. 1st Class Carriage. 1839. — Birmingham & Derby Junction. 2nd Class Carriage. 1839. — Midland Counties Railway. 3rd Class Carriage. 1842. — Midland Counties Railway. 2nd Class Carriage. 1844. — Mansfield & Pinxton Railway. 2nd & 3rd Class Compo. 1848. — 1st Class Carriage. 1848.

1st Class Carriage. 1848. — 2nd Class Carriage. 1848. — 3rd Class Carriage (Broad Gauge) 1848. — 2nd Class Carriage. 1858. — 1st & 2nd Class Compo. 1861.

3rd Class Carriage. 1865. — 1st Class Carriage. 1867. — 2nd Class Carriage. 1867. — Composite Carriage. 1874.

Plate 32.

Plate 33.

PRESIDENT'S ADDRESS.

Midland Passenger Vehicles. 1875 to 1897.

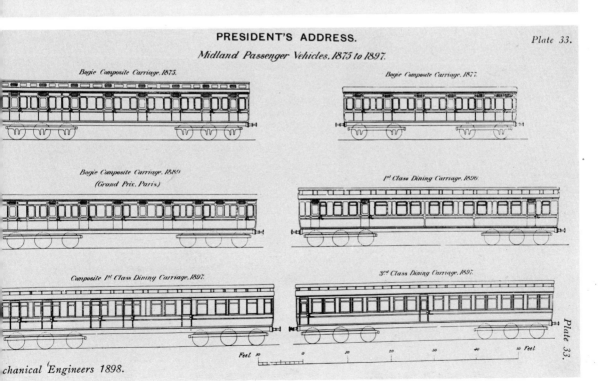

Bogie Composite Carriage. 1875. — Bogie Composite Carriage. 1877.

Bogie Composite Carriage. 1889. (Grand Prix, Paris) — 1st Class Dining Carriage. 1896.

Composite 1st Class Dining Carriage. 1897. — 3rd Class Dining Carriage. 1897.

Plate 33.

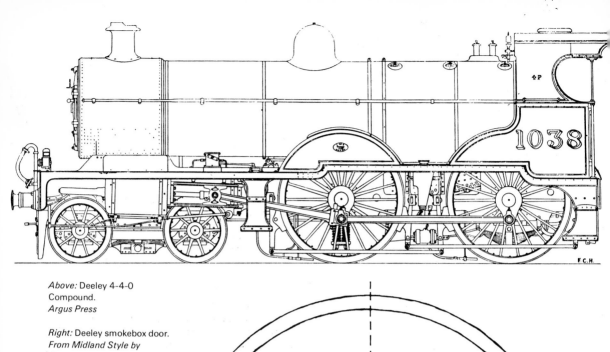

Above: Deeley 4-4-0
Compound.
Argus Press

Right: Deeley smokebox door.
*From Midland Style by
George Dow*

2717

24

6"

0   2 FEET

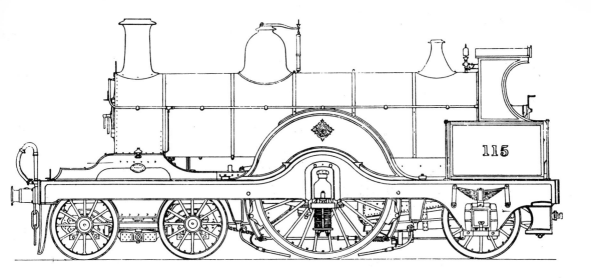

Above: Johnson 4-2-2. *Argus Press*

became the new Chief Mechanical Engineer, no doubt by then with a better appreciation of Deeley's point of view all those years before. Now it was Fowler who had unrealised projects for larger locomotives in the drawing office. With the extensive requirements of the LMS system and greatly increasing loads, the small engine policy began to look vulnerable. The crunch came when traffic requirements caused a new breed of 4-6-0, to be designed in a hurry in conjunction with the North British Locomotive Co. The resulting 3-cylinder 'Royal Scots' had a boiler based on the Midland Lickey banker, and the first batch consisted of 50 locomotives. A second batch of 20 locomotives was built by Derby, with boilers from Crewe, and completed from 1930 onwards. They were to bear the brunt of the West Coast main line traffic successfully until the coming of the Stanier Pacifics, and lasted for many years after following rebuilding by Stanier. Other locomotives of the Fowler regime were the LMS-built Compound 4-4-0s, the capable 4-6-0 3-cylinder 'Patriots' (or 'Baby Scots'), successful 2-6-4Ts, and the rather mundane 0-8-0s and 2-6-2Ts. It also saw the introduction of the 2-6-0+0-6-2 Beyer-Garratts for the heavy coal traffic from Toton.

In 1931, E. H. J. Lemon succeeded Sir Henry Fowler for a short period, but was then promoted to the post of Vice President in charge of Traffic and Operation. It was left to the man from Swindon, William Stanier appointed in 1932, to solve the conflicting loyalties of Derby, Crewe and Horwich and the

problems of the Motive Power Department and put a new imprint on LMS locomotive design.

When I first visited Derby Works in May 1934 the Stanier 3-cylinder taper boiler 2-6-4Ts eventually intended for the Southend line were under construction and due to be completed by the end of the year. Nos 2505/6 were at that time going through the paint shop and 2507/8, the erecting shops. As it turned out, I was to come to know these engines and some of their companions intimately three to four months later on the Midland main line between Radlett and St Pancras. In fact I was destined to see every member of this class of 37, there and elsewhere. They were capable and smooth running and have been likened to sewing machines.

In another part of the shop was a locomotive which had been built at Derby 20 years earlier, the Fowler outside-cylindered 2-8-0, Somerset & Dorset No 85, renumbered into LMS stock as No 13805. This was the engine originally tried out in 1918 to assess the suitability of the design for the Midland main line coal trains between Toton and London. However at the time there were loading gauge and bearing problems, so these fine locomotives never developed into a large class.

A unique occupant of the shops when I was at Derby, was that odd relation to the 'Royal Scot' class, the 4-6-0 experimental engine No 6399 *Fury*, which had arrived there for repairs, following its fatal accident at Carstairs in 1930 when a firebox super-pressure tube burst. This locomotive was virtually a 3-cylinder Compound with a German design Schmidt-Henschel triple-pressure boiler, at pressures of 1,400, 900 and 250lb/sq in respectively. It was a formidable machine, and I was able to see the layout of the controls. For the previous two years No 6399 had been making periodic test runs with a dynamometer car between Derby and Trent, Wellingboro' and Leicester. Its last run to Trent had been made two months before my visit, in March. Some 500 miles had been covered, but a decision had been reached that further tests would be unproductive, and shortly after I saw it the engine left Derby for Crewe. There it was rebuilt as No 6170 *British Legion* and later became the prototype for the very successful rebuilt 'Scots'. A photograph of *Fury* taken in the paint shop at Derby sometime before 1932 shows that it appears to have been in the company of North London 4-4-0T No 6445 and a Midland Kirtley double framed 2-4-0. Contrasts in technology, none were destined to survive except No 6399 which provided the foundation for a new locomotive. The others were scrapped in a case of

lamentable shortsightedness (an echo of Swindon's treatment of the broad gauge *North Star*), when all the historic engines preserved at Derby were destroyed with the fortunate exception of Johnson single driver No 118 of the '115' class. This was one of the less happy episodes of Stanier's regime.

Two years after the holocaust, I was able to see the Midland 7ft $9\frac{1}{2}$in 4-2-2 in the Derby works 'museum', in the company of the LNW saloon of 1869 for Queen Victoria. This famous carriage is now in the National Railway Museum at York.

The Johnson 'spinner' started life in 1897 as No 118, it was then renumbered 673 in 1907 and retained that number when it became part of the LMS locomotive stock in 1923. Withdrawn five years later, one of its final sheds being Birmingham, it was kept at Derby, being brought out for special occasions such as the Liverpool Centenary Exhibition in 1930. When I saw it at the works 'museum' it had been repainted in its original Midland livery and renumbered back to 118. Its chimney appeared to be in its original Johnson

Below: 'An engine is wheeled', British Rail poster of Derby Works by Terence Cuneo.
Crown Copyright, National Railway Museum, York

DERBY LOCOMOTIVE WORKS
AN ENGINE IS WHEELED
BRITISH RAILWAYS   BRITISH RAILWAYS

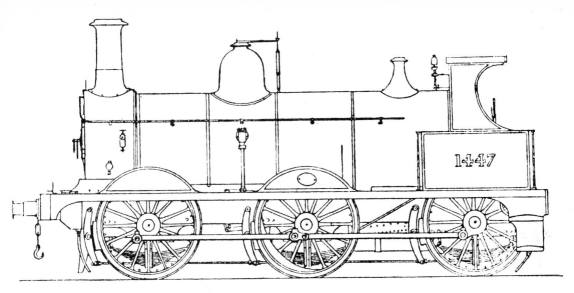

Above: Johnson 0-6-0. *Argus Press*

shape, but it may have been a replica. Years later the engine left Derby to go to the Stoneygate Museum at Leicester. More recently it has been repainted in its 1907 livery and is again No 673. It has since operated under its own steam at the Midland Railway Trust, Butterley, Derbyshire, in the company of Kirtley outside framed 2-4-0 No 158A, painted in pre-1907 Midland livery. The latter as No 20002 was withdrawn from active service in 1947, and had been kept at Derby for exhibition purposes. Originally built there in 1866, it is a worthy representative of a very long lived class, several of which I saw in service. In 1980 4-2-2 No 673 appeared in the 'Rocket 150' Cavalcade at Rainhill.

Time sets limits on what can be observed in the course of a visit, but in the shops in May 1934 were Johnson 0-4-4Ts Nos 1251/61/1303/40/82, Fowler Class 3 0-6-0T No 16710. 2-6-2Ts Nos 44/8/9, Fowler 2-6-4Ts Nos 2306/8/15/27, and Deeley 'flat iron' 0-6-4Ts Nos 2011/5/22. It is strange that these engines of uncertain reputation, for which Deeley himself originally considered the 2-6-4T wheel arrangement, can be said to have provided a basis for the very successful Fowler 2-6-4T locomotives (another influence was Horwich), and led to the long line of LMS 2-6-4Ts which culminated in the Riddles' version of British Rail days.

Midland Class 2 4-4-0s to be seen were Nos 364/ 76/94/415/507/18/38 and I recall that No 376 was of the straight footplate variety. Johnson Class 3 4-4-0 No 776 fitted with a Kylala blast pipe was in the paint shop and No 777 was in the erecting shops, together with Deeley Class 4 3-cylinder Compounds Nos 1009/ 42, and Johnson 0-6-0s Nos 3005/3189/3406/3585

with LMS Fowler Class 4 0-6-0 No 4434. Johnson 0-6-0 No 3642 and Fowler Class 4 No 4337 had reached the paint shop. Also in the erecting shops was Somerset & Dorset No 82, by then LMS No 13802.

On adjacent lines and in the sheds there was further variety, such as Kirtley well tank No 1212 bearing a notice 'To be kept at Derby', perhaps at the time preservation was under consideration. Originally numbered 1201, it had been renumbered in 1930 to make way for the S&DJR Johnson 0-4-4Ts incorporated into LMS stock. Johnson Midland 0-4-4Ts noted were Nos 1287/90/1322/75/98/1408/9/18/28/9 and Johnson 'brewery' 0-4-0ST No 1516, built sometime after 1883 and rebuilt in 1914. This particular engine was seen nearly 20 years later at Burton shed as No 41516. These locomotives were the original 'Jinties', a nickname derived I believe from the 'J' class boiler used in their construction.

Other engines recorded were 0-6-0Ts, Johnson Class 1 Nos 1690/1726/40/1839/45/65/73/96, Johnson Class 3 No 1953 and Fowler Class 3 Nos 7106/17/40, and a Deeley 0-6-4T No 2018. Midland Class 2 4-4-0s on shed were Nos 409/46/502/3/4/22/ 6/40, together with Johnson Class 3 4-4-0s Nos 717/ 44/75, Deeley Class 4 Compound No 1031, and LNW 4-6-0 'Claughton' No 5955 (LNW 1103) which I had seen earlier on the Midland main line at Luton. A last echo from the Midland era, but appearing under Stanier, was LMS 0-4-4T No 6409 with stove pipe chimney. Johnson and Fowler 0-6-0s included Class 3 No 3218, formerly S&DJR No 73. Their numbers were 2968/9/3062/4/8/83/96/8/3103/8/10/35/6/53/ 68/75/6/91/6/3200/25/9/31/41/7/51/64/3300/12/5/ 23/64/71/3438/40/3/5/3524/6/59/3603/24/37/91/ 3703/35/63/90/7/3811/24/6/33 and Fowler Class 4 Nos 3866/3908/42/74/4035/94/8/4133/5/59/4402/ 12/18/20/4501/59 (formerly S&DJR No 59).

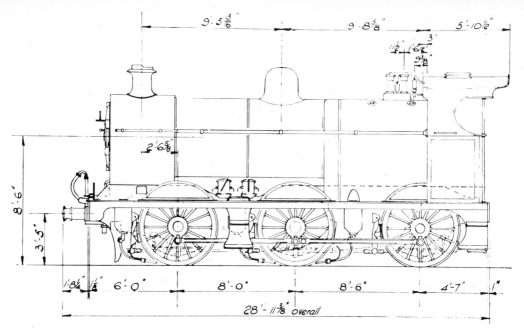

Above: Fowler 0-6-0.   *Railway Modeller*

October 1935 saw me once again at Derby, in time to see a rare locomotive I had noted in April 1934 at Plaistow shed, now unfortunately in the Works for scrapping. This was one of the four 4-4-2Ts fitted with condensing apparatus and rounded cabs by the London, Tilbury & Southend Railway for working through the underground tunnels of the Whitechapel & Bow Railway. It was originally No 3 *Tilbury*, one of the first batch of LTS engines delivered by Sharp Stewart in 1880, having at that time a stove-pipe chimney, a feature that showed its Adams ancestry. Although No 2079 as it now was, probably retained its condensing gear later than its companions, this had all gone when I saw it at Derby. There were also two others of the original LTS 4-4-2Ts built by Sharp Stewart, in for scrapping, No 2078 constructed in 1880 as No 2 *Gravesend*, and No 2076 built in 1884 as No 25 *Stifford*.

In service at Derby from Peterborough shed was Johnson 6ft 9in 2-4-0 No 269. Other locomotives were Midland Class 2 4-4-0s Nos 382/97/408/25/55/95-97/501-4/13/6/25/6/46 and LMS No 630. No 502 was on an inspection saloon. I noted four Johnson Class 3 4-4-0s Nos 748/74/5/6 and Deeley Class 4 Compound 4-4-0s Nos 1000/4/10/14/26/44 Fowler LMS Nos 1046/8/9/57/8/9/61/2/74/96/1105/7/73. There were also Hughes 2-6-0s Nos 13193, 2798/2846, Stanier Class 5 4-6-0s Nos 5031/66 and Class 5XP 'Jubilee' Nos 5618/29/38. In the freight category were Kirtley double framed 0-6-0s Nos 22822/49, Johnson 0-6-0s Nos 22933/47/65/79/82 (all these

engines had 20000 added in 1934)/3000/1/18/3108/9/16/23/53/66/85/87/98/3200/14/29/47/3312/55/64/70/4/82/3400/16/32/40/3/5/6/94/6/3530/53/3603/29/82/96/3723/45/55/7/63/74/91/3824/30, Fowler Class 4 0-6-0s Nos 3839/47/52/5/6/3939/41/65/72/5/90, LMS Fowler 0-6-0s Nos 4032/5/91/2/7/4101/4/36/57/8/77/4245/49/93/4334/7/61/4402/14/19/26/31/4552. No 4414 was fitted with a staff catcher. Other Fowler engines were 7F 0-8-0s Nos 9514/5/32/81/9627 and S&D 2-8-0s Nos 13801/5 (home shed Bath), formerly Nos 81 and 85 respectively. When taken into LMS stock in 1930 the 2-8-0s were originally numbered 9670-80, but in 1932 were renumbered 13800-10 to allow for the last batch of Fowler 0-8-0s. I also noted Beyer-Garratt 2-6-0+0-6-2 No 4990, one of the second batch with increased bunker capacity, and finally fitted with rotating bunkers in 1932-3. The motion of these locomotives was based on that of the S&DJR 2-8-0s. LNW visitors were Bowen Cooke 'G1' 0-8-0s Nos 9209 (734)/9218 (1343) and Beames 'G2' 0-8-0 No 9450 (13).

Tank engines I recall were Johnson 0-4-4Ts No 1238 (of the 1236-65 batch with 5ft 7in driving wheels, the rest having 5ft 4in)/1293/1327/56/1425/8/9, Fowler 2-6-2Ts Nos 23/49/60, Stanier 2-6-2Ts Nos 114/38, Deeley 0-6-4Ts Nos 2032/4, Fowler 2-6-4Ts Nos 2311/6/38/66, LTS Class 2 4-4-2T No 2093 (formerly No 52 *Wennington*) Johnson Class 1 0-6-0Ts Nos 1795/1804/16/31/3/9/65/73/6, Johnson Class 3 0-6-0Ts Nos 1920/7223, Fowler Class 3 0-6-0Ts Nos 7100/5/7/16761 (being renumbered 7678), Johnson 0-4-0ST No 1509 (with bell) and Deeley 0-4-0 side tank No 1532. Both were classified OF.

Above: Kirtley double framed (curved frames over coupling-rod cranks) 0-6-0 No 22852 of the series built between 1863 and 1874. Rebuilt by Johnson and Deeley, with new cab, and Belpaire firebox as part of Class 2 boiler. Although having 20,000 added to its number in 1934, it is still in its pre-1928 livery with painted LMS plate on cab side and numbers on tender at Derby in 1934. *Author*

Below: Johnson Class 2 0-6-0 No 3438 of the series built 1875-1908 with 4ft 11in or 5ft 3in driving wheels, the engine belonging to the latter series. Rebuilt with Belpaire boiler, and on Derby shed in 1934. *Author*

Above: At Derby shed in 1934, Johnson Class 2 0-6-0 No 3691, rebuilt with Belpaire boiler. *Author*

Right: Large boilered Fowler S&DJR 2-8-0 No 87, built by Robert Stephenson in 1925, with its final number after being taken into LMS stock of 13807, in Derby repair shop in 1933 and attached to Bristol shed. *H. C. Casserley*

Below: The last of the smaller boilered S&DJR 2-8-0s No 85 built at Derby in 1915, on test on the Midland main line in 1918 with a view to use for the Toton coal traffic. No 85 was in the Derby paint shop in 1934 with its final LMS No 13805. *H. C. Casserley*

Bottom: Deeley Class 3 0-6-4T No 2026 built 1907 and rebuilt with Belpaire boiler and superheater in 1924, at Derby in 1934 from Birmingham shed. *Author*

Below: Deeley Class 3 0-6-4T No 2008 built 1907 and rebuilt with Belpaire boiler and superheater in early 1920s, together with Johnson 0-6-0 No 3827 rebuilt with Class 3 Belpaire boiler and Deeley cab, at Derby. *Author*

Bottom: Whitelegg Class 3 4-4-2T No 2143 (LTSR No 45 *Shoeburyness*) shedded at Derby in 1937. *H. C. Casserley*

Above: Johnson 'brewery' tank engine No 1518 with stovepipe chimney (these were the original 'Jinties') of the series built between 1883 and 1903. Smokebox of newly painted former Somerset & Dorset 2-8-0 No 13802 on right, at Derby. *S. F. Hull*

Below: Designed while E. J. H. Lemon was acting CME, and the last 'Midland' conception, but built under Stanier, LMS Class 2 0-4-4T No 6409 built 1932 with stovepipe chimney, and LMS 3-cylinder Compound 4-4-0 No 1075 built Derby 1924 and bearing Carlisle shed plate. *Author*

Above: Johnson 4-2-2 with 7ft 9½in driving wheels, No 673 and the last Midland single in regular service was withdrawn in 1928, and preserved at Derby, repainted in its original MR livery and number of 118. It was built at Derby Works in 1897 and was a member of the '115' class. Brought out for special occasions, it was at the Liverpool Centenary Exhibition in 1930, and was seen in 1934 in a disused paint shop at Derby, still with its original Johnson design of chimney (believed to be a replica), in company with the LNWR saloon for Queen Victoria which was formed from two 6-wheelers built in 1869, into a coach with 6-wheel bogies, and later went to the National Railway Museum. *LPC*

Above right: Johnson 4-2-2 No 118 repainted to Midland Deeley livery and numbered once again 673, provided with Deeley chimney, and loaned by the National Railway Museum to the Midland Railway Trust at Butterley. Back in full working order, No 673 took part in the 'Rocket 150' celebrations at Rainhall in 1980. *F. Ashley/IAL*

Right: Class 6 3-cylinder Compound 4-6-0 experimental high pressure engine No 6399 *Fury* built 1929 by North British Locomotive Co, with Schmidt-Henschel triple-pressure boiler with three units generating steam at 1,400, 900 and 250lb/sq in respectively. Following explosion of a firebox super pressure tube the locomotive was sent to Derby, where it was stored in the paint shop, incidentally in company with the North London Railway 4-4-0T which was unfortunately not preserved. *Fury* was again steamed and underwent another series of tests, coal consumption proving unsatisfactory. *Modern Transport*

Above: In 1935 No 6399 was rebuilt at Crewe with a Stanier taper boiler and normal 3-cylinder simple layout. It was renumbered 6170 and named *British Legion*, forming in many respects a prototype for the later rebuilding of the 'Royal Scots' with taper boilers.   *W. Potter/IAL*

Below: In 1932 Derby constructed its first diesel locomotive by rebuilding Johnson Class 1 0-6-0T No 1831 and fitting with a Paxman 6-cylinder diesel engine with hydrostatic transmission.

Down the Thames Estuary

In 1912, the Midland absorbed the London, Tilbury & Southend Railway, much to the disgust of the Great Eastern which regarded the acquisition as an assault on its territory. It should not have been surprised; for although in the early days the LTSR had close links with the GER and part of Fenchurch Street station was leased from the latter, there had long been a useful liaison with the Midland, ever since the Tottenham & Hampstead and Tottenham & Forest Gate joint railways came into being, the latter in 1894.

One year after the opening of the through route provided by these joint railways a regular train service commenced between St Pancras and Southend worked by Midland engines. In 1899 these were superseded by LTSR locomotives, but specials continued to be worked by the Midland. One of that railway's rare named engines, the famous Johnson 4-4-0 *Beatrice* had been stationed at Shoeburyness with other MR locomotives for working the expresses between Southend and St Pancras. After 1899 some LTS engines were shedded at Kentish Town, dual fitted with vacuum brakes to work Midland stock, the LTSR being a Westinghouse line. The first to arrive was Class 1 4-4-2T No 5 *Plaistow* to be followed by Nos 4, 8, 10 and 28. They were in due course replaced by the Class 2 Intermediate 4-4-2Ts, which worked the service for many years. After the Midland took over the LTS in 1912, the only 4-4-2T to remain at Kentish Town was No 61 named appropriately *Kentish Town*. This was the engine that had achieved fame for its elaborate decorations in 1902 for the coronation of King Edward VII.

Right from the opening of the Forest Gate line the Midland maintained a regular suburban service between St Pancras and East Ham. There were also many freight workings by the Midland over the GER to the Thames Docks. Nor should it be forgotten that the latter railway had running powers which it exercised for many years into St Pancras, working through expresses and these powers were retained by their successors the LNER, although not exercised, at least to my knowledge. However as late as 1922 a GE express was run between St Pancras and Hunstanton.

It will be seen that the St Pancras-Southend con-

nection was of very long standing between the Midland and LTS and this continued to thrive in LMS days. There were through boat trains to Tilbury Docks, and apart from the ordinary train service there were many excursions. In fact my earliest acquaintance with the LTSR was on a Midland excursion in 1919 from Harringay Park. In the 1920s, I travelled in these trains on a number of occasions. They were normally composed of Bain compartment stock and hauled by Fowler Class 4 0-6-0s, and were heavily loaded with Londoners on the day out. Another type to be seen at Southend were Hughes 2-6-0s on excursion trains from places down the main line.

A line which had a close association with the LTS was the North London, whose 4-4-0Ts used to work through excursions to Southend, until some of the 'Tilbury' Class 1 4-4-2Ts were vacuum fitted. The other link was with the District Railway via the Whitechapel & Bow for which four LTS Class 1 4-4-2Ts were modified with condensing apparatus and round profiled cab roofs. I saw three of them, No 2083 (No 7 *Barking*) at Broad Street on the North London with the apparatus in situ, No 2059 (No 29 *Stepney*) at Upminster, and No 2079 (No 3 *Tilbury*) at Derby in 1935 with the apparatus removed.

After electrification of the District and Whitechapel & Bow, through trains to Southend of LTS stock were worked between Ealing and Barking by two District electric locomotives, formerly used on the old Outer Circle trains. From there they were taken over by LTS 4-4-2Ts or later the 4-6-4Ts of Robert Whitelegg. Two special trains of saloon, lavatory stock were built by the LTS for this service and I recall travelling in these over the District.

Before the take-over, LTS engines were painted green, and Midlandisation meant crimson lake for passenger locomotives and black for goods. Large numerals replaced the names on tank sides, a few engines receiving them while retaining the old livery. Derby chimneys and other fittings gradually appeared. Midland 2-4-0s, 4-4-0s, 0-6-0s, 0-4-4Ts, and Deeley 0-6-4Ts for a time, became part of the scene, together with a Johnson 4-2-2 on an inspection saloon. LTS

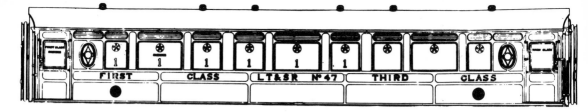

Above: LTSR special stock for Ealing-Southend through trains.
From Midland Style by George Dow,
drawn by Andrew Ivor Dunbar

0-6-2Ts worked goods trains over the Tottenham joint lines to Cricklewood on the Midland main line, and Derby 0-6-0s travelled down to Tilbury Docks.

In the 1920s and 1930s, 'Tilbury' tank engines were seen in a variety of 'locales', not only in the immediate London area but further afield. The Whitelegg 4-6-4Ts Nos 2196/8 could be seen at St Pancras or Kentish Town in the earlier part of the period and I was hauled by them on a number of occasions. The class 1, 2 and 3 4-4-2Ts often came into Broad Street and I recall the following engines, Class 1 Nos 2058/60/1/3/7/75/8/80/3(condensing)/90, Class 2 Nos 2092-2102/4/7-9, Class 3 Nos 2135-7/48(80 *Thundersley*, now preserved)/50, LMS Class 3 Nos 2110-12/6/24/6-29/51/8.

LTS 4-4-2s Nos 2105/37/40 and LMS version Nos 2118/9 I saw at St Pancras, while out on the main line near Radlett I recorded Class 2 No 2102 and LMS Class 3 No 2111. 'Tilbury' tanks had worked on the St Albans trains and some migrated further north to places like Nottingham, and Leicester where I saw Class 2 No 2093 (formerly No 52 *Wennington*).

Plaistow was not only a shed but had been the works of the LTSR. It was while planning these works that the then manager and resident engineer, Arthur Stride, was asked by his board to seek the advice of William Adams regarding suitable tank engines for the railway. Adams whose former career as locomotive superintendent had been with the North London and Great Eastern Railways, was at that time in a similar capacity with the London & South Western. The resulting proposal was a free running 4-4-2T related to the 4-4-0T designs which Adams had produced for the NL and LSW railways. Originally, needless to say, fitted with stove-pipe chimneys, the locomotives proved to be the commencement of a long line of tank engines extending into LMS days. Not only that, Adams's former assistant at the Great Eastern, Thomas Whitelegg, was appointed to be the first locomotive superintendent of the LTSR. It ultimately proved to be a family affair as his son Robert succeeded to the post in 1910 designing the large 4-6-4Ts and after the Midland took over, moving on after an interval to the Glasgow & South Western Railway in 1918 where he amplified the type.

When I went to Plaistow shed (MR 34/LMS 13A) in 1934, I recall the following engines: Class 1 4-4-2Ts Nos 2067/70/2/3/9 (condensing engine for the Whitechapel & Bow and seen at Derby in 1935 for scrapping) 2090, Class 2 4-4-2Ts Nos 2093/8/2109 (nicknamed 'the camel' because the addition of an experimental top feed had resulted in two domes), Class 3 4-4-2Ts Nos 2141 (from Tilbury)/2/5, LTS 0-6-2Ts Class 2F Nos 2223/4/8-30/3, Johnson 0-6-0 No 3049, Class 1 0-6-0T No 1718, Class 3 No 1951.

The Midland inherited a useful fleet of solidly constructed bogie carriages with semi-elliptical roofs from the 'Tilbury'. They were finished in varnished teak externally, which they retained for some time being merely relettered and renumbered by the Midland. They were all compartment carriages apart from the special saloon rolling stock which was designed for use on the through trains between Ealing on the District and Southend and had through gangways, with toilets in the brake thirds. Some of the ordinary carriages also had toilets, which were between compartments.

There was one unusual coach which should be mentioned: completed in 1913 at Plaistow it was probably intended to be a directors' saloon. Designed by Robert Whitelegg, it contained a lounge, smoking and dining compartments, pantry and a lavatory. Appearing just after the line was taken over by the Midland, it had the unusual distinction of being finished in varnished teak, but it had the MR coat of arms on the sides and was lettered MR in a flowing script. It retained its livery well into LMS days and I was fortunate to see this vehicle, as far as I can recall, at St Pancras.

Both the Midland and LMS built stock for the LTS. In 1915 David Bain built two sets of 13 carriages each, comprising low arc roofed, compartment lavatory fitted stock with wide bodies. Similar carriages were incorporated in the make-up of some of the LTS sets. From 1924 onwards R. W. Reid, Bain's successor at the Midland and by then LMS Carriage & Wagon Superintendent, initiated a number of 11-coach sets with lavatory compartments for the LTS section. Bearing set numbers from F&S 241 to F&S 265 (F&S: Fenchurch Street & Southend) the majority were built at Derby, and were of basically Midland design, the early sets having that railway's fittings.

Above: LTS section Class 1 4-4-2T No 2079 as built in 1880 as LTSR No 3 *Tilbury*, one of the original batch of 12 engines with small dome and stove-pipe chimney.

Centre left: Class 1 4-4-2Ts LTSR Nos 3, 7, 23 and 29 were later given shortened chimneys, rounded cabs, condensing gear and Westinghouse feed-water pumps for working in the tunnels of the Whitechapel & Bow Railway, No 3 as LMS No 2079 was seen at Derby in 1935 preparatory to being scrapped.

Bottom left: LTS section Class 2 4-4-2T No 2107 near Leigh-on-Sea. Originally LTSR '51' class No 66 *Earls Court*. Midland Railway warning notice on left. *Author*

Right: LTS section Class 2 4-4-2T, LTSR '51' class built 1900-3 on up working from Tilbury line to Broad Street station passing Shoreditch on the North London. Probably boat train stock, with LNWR bogie elliptical roofed luggage van behind engine. *Author*

Below: In 1909 four large 4-4-2Ts, known as the '79' class were introduced by the LTSR and constructed by Robert Stephenson & Co. They were the last to be built before the Midland took over in 1912. LTSR No 82 *Crowstone* of the class, as LMS Class 3 No 2150 after rebuilding with Derby fittings. Another engine of this class No 80 *Thundersley* is preserved in semi-original condition. *Author*

Right: Class 3 4-4-2T on heavy up train to Fenchurch Street, near Leigh-on-Sea. *Author*

Below: LTS section Class 3 4-4-2T No 2113. This was one of the 10 engines with Midland modifications, of the '79' class ordered from Derby in 1922. Appearing in 1923, the first eight Nos 2110-17 had the Midland crest and date plates although the LMS had just come into existence. *Author*

Above: Further Class 3 4-4-2Ts were ordered by the LMS and built in 1925, 1927 and 1930. No 2124 was the last engine of the 1925 order. *Author*

Below: LMS Class 3 4-4-2T No 2153 built in 1930 and one of the last batch to be constructed, on Fenchurch Street-Southend train in 1936. *E. R. Wethersett/IAL*

Above: Another of the 1930 batch, LMS Class 2 4-4-2T No 2152 of Plaistow shed at St Pancras about 1934. *C. R. L. Coles*

Centre left: At West Ham shed, one of the first series of LTSR 0-6-2Ts No 70 *Basildon* built 1903, as LMS No 2221 with Derby fittings.

Bottom left: One of the second series of LTSR 0-6-2Ts, No 2227 built 1908 and originally LTSR No 76 *Dunton*. *Author*

Above: LMS Class 2 0-6-2T No 2230, the first of the third series of LTSR 0-6-2Ts built 1912, which never bore its LTS number but went straight into Midland stock as No 2190. *Author*

Centre right: The last LTSR design was eight 4-6-4Ts or 'Baltics', designed by Robert Whitelegg, son of Thomas Whitelegg who served the LTSR as Locomotive Superintendent from 1880-1910. Appearing in 1912 they never received their LTS numbers and went straight into Midland stock. Unfortunately their weight precluded them from operating into Fenchurch Street, and one of their duties became working the through Ealing-Southend trains, where they took over from the District electric locomotives at Barking.

Bottom right: LTS 4-6-4T, LMS No 2196 with Derby modifications at St Pancras in the early 1930s. *Author*

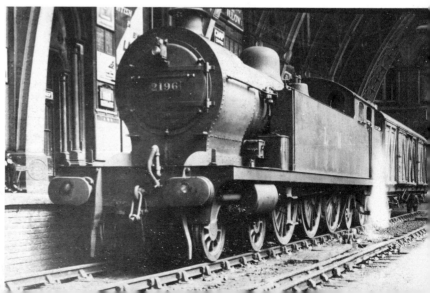

Above: LTS 4-6-4T No 2196 from Kentish Town shed on St Pancras-St Albans train near Elstree in 1931. *H. C. Casserley*

Below: The Stanier 3-cylinder 2-6-4Ts, which were designed with the LTS section in mind, did not go there directly at least as far as the earlier engines were concerned, both the St Pancras-St Albans-Luton service on the Midland main line receiving a number, together with the Western division outer suburban services from Euston. The first of the class No 2500 built 1934, and observed at Euston in that year, seen here passing Westcliff on up Fenchurch Street train in 1936. *E. R. Wethersett/IAL*

Above: Stanier Class 4 2-6-4T No 2524 built 1934, at Plaistow shed in 1935. Nos 2500-9 had straight bunker tops instead of sloping, and from No 2525 onwards the cab sides were slightly modified with a rear cutaway. *E. R. Wethersett/IAL*

Below: Passing Leigh on up train at Upminster in 1936, Stanier 2-6-4T No 2525, showing cutaway cab side. *E. R. Wethersett/IAL*

Top left: Up train from Shoeburyness leaving Southend East in 1936 with Stanier 2-6-4T No 2531 of Shoeburyness shed. In the mid-1930s these locomotives could often be seen at St Pancras, as was No 2531 in 1935. *E. R. Wethersett/IAL*

Left: Southend train at St Pancras with Midland Class 4 0-6-0 No 3938, one of the batch built by Armstrong-Whitworth in 1921-22. These workings were in operation long before the LTSR became part of the Midland. In the 1920s and 1930s the Fowler Class 4 0-6-0s were often rostered for this duty, particularly where excursions were concerned. *Author*

Above: Fowler Class 4 0-6-0 No 4298 of Cricklewood shed on down excursion from the Midland in 1936. These trains were often very heavily loaded, Southend being a popular resort for Londoners, aided by attractive cheap fares.
E. R. Wethersett/IAL

Above: Hughes/Fowler 2-6-0 No 2870 of Kentish Town shed on Southend excursion, with Midland low-arc roofed suburban stock, in the mid-1930s. *Author*

Below: Near Leigh, Stanier Class 5 4-6-0 No 5053 on 13 coach Southend-St Pancras train in 1936. *E. R. Wethersett/IAL*

Bottom: The unique saloon carriage designed by Robert Whitelegg, probably for the directors of the LTSR, but overtaken by the merger with the Midland Railway in 1912. Exterior finished in LTS livery of varnished teak, but with Midland coat of arms and lettered MR in flowing script. Retaining its livery well into LMS days, it is thought to have been used as a special saloon on boat trains. *LPC*

Into East Anglia

Unlike the London, Tilbury & Southend which spent its nursery years with Great Eastern blessing, the Eastern & Midlands Railway Co had to put up a fight to establish itself in East Anglia, taking over a number of smaller lines in the process. By 1893, Derby and Kings Cross had moved in on the scene and the Eastern & Midlands was embodied in the Midland & Great Northern Joint Committee with three Midland and three GN directors. Through trains began to be operated from the midlands and the south to Cromer, Norwich, Yarmouth and the Norfolk broads. Peace was settled with the GER to the extent that the Joint Committee became co-owners with the latter of the Norfolk & Suffolk Joint Railway, the various portions of which were built in the years 1898, 1903 and 1906. The places served among others were North Walsham, Mundesley, Cromer Beach, Yarmouth and Lowestoft.

In point of mileage the M&GN was the largest joint railway in Britain and had its own workshops at Melton Constable, a central point on the system. Among an interesting stock of locomotives it had outside cylinder 4-4-0s from Beyer Peacock & Co and typical Midland 4-4-0s and 0-6-0s to Samuel Johnson's design, the latter being responsible for motive power to the Joint Committee in the earlier part of the lines existence. William Marriott from the Eastern & Midlands was in charge at Melton Constable as Engineer and Locomotive Superintendent up until 1924, and between 1904 and 1910 three personable outside cylinder 4-4-2Ts were constructed. There were also some neat outside cylinder 0-6-0Ts of unlikely origin, having been built from parts of engines from the Cornish Minerals Railway. Curiously these little engines turned out to be very long lived, two of them lasting until nationalisation. Apart from the Johnson and Marriott influences there were a number of 0-6-0s of H. A. Ivatt's design for the Great Northern and diverted to the stock of the M&GN by that railway.

At one time the Midland brought in some Johnson 0-4-4Ts and later the LMS introduced three of the Class 3 Johnson 4-4-0s which proved popular with M&GN drivers. At the end of 1936, the LNER took over the motive power of the joint line and among new types introduced were the GER 'B12' 4-6-0s as rebuilt by Gresley to Class B12/3.

M&GN carriages were of Great Northern 6-wheel design and finished in varnished teak. These were later reinforced by the LMS with ex-MR and LNW bogie stock and by the LNE with NER and still later, GER bogie carriages. Up until 1929 engines were painted a golden ochre colour for passenger work, the goods locomotives having gone over to a dark brown, lined yellow about 1923. By the time I knew the M&GN in 1933 they were all dark brown, many with Johnson style raised brass numerals on the cab sides. The stations I recall were painted in a warm combination of cream and ochre colours.

With its long stretches of single track through the Norfolk countryside, there would be periods of silence on the M&GN, punctuated by the sound of an occasional heavy train of agricultural produce, then a series of passenger trains one after the other especially on summer Saturdays when heavy holiday traffic, a lot of it from the Midlands, was in evidence. Agriculture and holiday makers were two important assets to the line, which in some respects was an English version of the Highland Railway, although in very different surroundings. A feature they had in common was automatic tablet exchange.

In 1933 when it was still its own master, I travelled behind most types of M&GN passenger locomotive and one Johnson goods 0-6-0, as well on the LNER Sentinel steam railcar No 248 *Tantivy* which was working on the M&GN. I recall seeing Beyer Peacock 6ft 0in 4-4-0s with outside cylinders and rebuilt with Midland boilers, Nos 24/9/31-4, and I was hauled by each of them at different times. The Johnson 4-4-0s both Class 1 and 2 with various rebuildings had close cousins on the Midland. Engines noted were Nos 1/6/11/2/6/7/36/7/9/45/9/51/2/75/8/9, and I was hauled by Nos 1/6. Johnson 0-6-0s, comparable with their Derby cousins, but built by Nielson & Co, seen were Nos 61/5/6 (which I had on a passenger train) 7/70/2. I was hauled from Mundesley to Cromer by Marriott outside cylinder 4-4-2T No 20 and noted No 41 at North Walsham. These engines had the same driving wheel dimension, 6ft 0in as the Class 1 'Tilbury' tanks and the same boiler pressure 160lbs/sq in. The M&GN locomotives had cylinders $17\frac{1}{2}$in × 24in, half inch larger in diameter and two inches shorter in stroke, the motion being interchangeable with the Beyer Peacock outside cylinder 4-4-0s. Also outside-cylindered were the small 0-6-0Ts with hopper bunkers Nos 15 and 97 seen at Yarmouth. At Cromer, one Ivatt GN representative with 0-6-0 No 88, designated Class 2.

Right: Midland & Great Northern Joint Railway Class A Beyer Peacock 4-4-0 No 34 built 1888 and reboilered with Midland 'C' type boiler and extended smokebox in 1908, at Cromer Beach in 1933. Typical M&GN 6-wheel carriages of GN design and finished in varnished teak, in background. *Author*

Below: M&GN Class C Johnson 4-4-0 No 6 built 1894, and rebuilt in 1930 with Midland G6 boiler and extended smokebox. *Author*

Above: By the coaling tower at Yarmouth Beach in 1933, M&GN Class C Johnson 4-4-0 No 51 built 1896 and rebuilt with Midland G7 boiler in 1915 with Deeley fittings. *Author*

Below: M&GN Class A Tank 4-4-2T No 20 built 1909 at Melton Constable, one of three constructed by the Locomotive Superintendent, William Marriott, and rebuilt in 1931. These were related to the Class A 4-4-0s. *Author*

Top: M&GN Class D Johnson 0-6-0 built 1896 by Neilson & Co and rebuilt in 1920. These engines were sometimes used on passenger trains. *Author*

Above: On normal goods duty, M&GN Class D Johnson 0-6-0 No 72, built 1899 by Kitson & Co and rebuilt 1920. *Author*

Northern Ireland

The Midland crossed the Irish Sea in 1903 and acquired the Belfast & Northern Counties Railway of mainly 5ft 3in gauge, forming the Northern Counties Committee, known as the NCC. With its main terminus and works at York Road, Belfast, it was a substantial and fairly prosperous system serving places such as Larne, Antrim, Ballymena, Coleraine, Portrush and Londonderry.

It also possessed an enterprising locomotive superintendent, Bowman Malcolm and it was not until the Midland became part of the LMS in 1923, that the NCC locomotive department really began to feel the influence of Derby. Locomotive rebuildings brought Midland features, extended smokeboxes, Belpaire fireboxes and new cabs, and most of Malcolm's successful 2-cylinder compounds on the Worsdell von Borries principle were converted to simples. In 1933, Derby introduced the first of a new class of 15 engines, the Class W 2-6-0s with 6ft 0in driving wheels which has features in common with the LMS Fowler 2-6-4Ts (their actual descendants, although they had a number of differences, could be seen with the Ivatt Class WT 2-6-4Ts which came to the NCC from Derby in 1946/7).

I saw several of the Class W 2-6-0s at York Road when I was in Belfast in 1936, No 92 *The Bann* at the head of a train waiting to depart to Portrush, No 90 *The Duke of Abercorn*, both of the first batch, and the later engines No 96 *Silver Jubilee* and No 97 *Earl of Ulster*.

Seawards on the north side of Belfast Lough is the seaside resort of Whitehead served by the NCC. Its former excursion platforms are now the centre of activities for the Railway Preservation Society of Ireland and their steam hauled excursions all over Ireland. Among a fine collection of operational locomotives they possess LMS (NCC) Class WT 2-6-4T No 4 which is reputed to have been the last main line steam locomotive on regular service in the British Isles. It has been working hard for the RPSI ever since, having been as far afield as Cork, Limerick and Galway, quite apart from being the regular engine on a train called the *Portrush Flyer*.

Back in June 1936 I was hauled from Belfast by Class B3 4-4-0 No 60 *County Donegal*, travelling in Midland design corridor carriage No 234, on a run well within schedule to Whitehead. While at the station I recall Class B3 4-4-0s Nos 24 *County Londonderry* and 28 *County Tyrone*, Class U2 4-4-0s Nos 75 *Antrim Castle* and 80 *Dunseverick Castle*. I returned to Belfast behind Class A1 4-4-0 No 33 *Binevenagh*. The carriage I travelled in was a LMS flush window, the smoking compartment having red 'leather' upholstery, black and white photographs depicting NCC resorts above the back of the seating and a map of the system. When we stopped at Carrickfergus I noted Class A1 4-4-0 No 69 *Slieve Bane* on a down train. All the locomotives I saw were in crimson lake with polished brass number and name plates, the latter certainly not a Midland tradition.

Other engines to be seen at various points were Class U1 4-4-0 No 4 *Glenariff*, Class U2 4-4-0 No 77 (unnamed), Class C1 Malcolm 'Worsdell von Borries' 2-cylinder Compound 2-4-0 No 57 *Galgorm Castle* and Class K1 0-6-0 No 43. At York Road station there were two railcars, No 1 built 1933 with two petrol engines and No 2 built 1934 with two diesel engines, part aluminium body and raised lookouts for the driver. There was also railcar Trailer No 1, one of two built in 1934.

Below: LMS/NCC Afternoon Excursion ticket, Belfast-Whitehead, 1936. *Author*

Left: LMS Northern Counties Committee 4-4-0 No 60 *County Donegal* on a train to Larne at York Road station, Belfast in 1936. *Author*

Below: NCC 4-4-0 No 69 *Slieve Bane* with LMS emblem on upper panel of cab side, showing typical Derby influences, on down train from Belfast terminating at Carrickfergus. *Author*

Right: Train for Larne at Whitehead in 1936 with NCC 4-4-0 No 28 *County Tyrone*. Derby boiler, cab and fittings. *Author*

Below right: Showing the combination of Derby and Belfast & Northern Counties practice, NCC No 60 *County Donegal* on Larne train at Whitehead in 1936. *Author*

Above: NCC 2-6-0 No 92 *The Bann*, one of the four built at
Derby in 1933 with boilers from Crewe. These engines were
related to the '2300' series of Fowler 2-6-4Ts, and further
engines of the type were built for the NCC. Note the top feed, a
sign of Stanier influence. At York Road station, Belfast, in
1936. *Author*

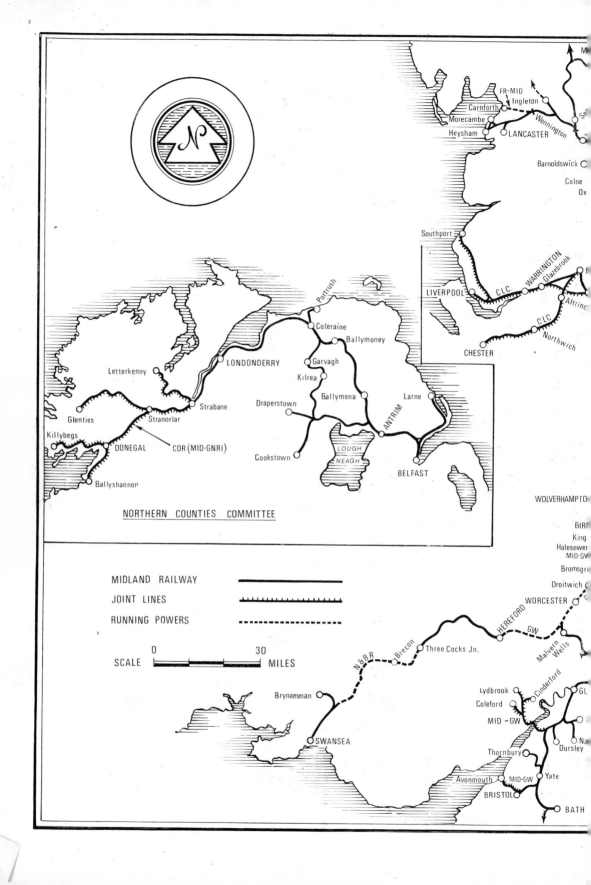

NORTHERN COUNTIES COMMITTEE

MIDLAND RAILWAY ————
JOINT LINES ╌╌╌╌╌╌╌
RUNNING POWERS ▪▪▪▪▪▪▪

SCALE 0 ▬▬▬ 30 MILES

FR-MID
Ingleton
Carnforth
Morecambe
Heysham
LANCASTER
Wennington
Se

Barnoldswick
Colne
Ox

Southport
LIVERPOOL
WARRINGTON
Glazebrook
C.L.C.
Altrinc
C.L.C.
Northwich
CHESTER

Portrush
Coleraine
Ballymoney
Garvagh
Kilrea
LONDONDERRY
Letterkenny
Draperstown
Ballymena
Larne
Strabane
ANTRIM
Glenties
Stranorlar
CDR (MID·GNRI)
Killybegs
DONEGAL
Cookstown
LOUGH NEAGH
BELFAST
Ballyshannon

WOLVERHAMPTO

BIR
King
Halesower
MID·GV
Bromsgr
Droitwich
WORCESTER
HEREFORD
GW
Three Cocks Jn.
Brecon
Malvern Wells
N&B·R
Lydbrook
Cinderford
Coleford
GL
MID·GW
Brynamman
Na
Dursley
Thornbury
SWANSEA
Avonmouth
MID·GW
Yate
BRISTOL
BATH